HOW TEACHERS CAN TURN DATA INTO ACTION

[redacted]

Praise for *How Teachers Can Turn Data into Action*

How Teachers Can Turn Data into Action is a relevant, hands-on resource that will help teacher teams—particularly those new to evidence-based instructional decision making—untangle thorny instructional challenges, improve classroom practice, and, ultimately, achieve results.

Dr. Naomi Cooperman, Director of Program Design,
Teaching Matters, New York, NY

Just days after first working with the Data Action Model, our faculty members started having their most productive and meaningful data analysis meetings to date. Using this model is clearly strengthening our learning organization.

Andrew Williams, Director of Curriculum,
Morris School District, Morristown, NJ

DANIEL R. VENABLES

HOW TEACHERS CAN TURN DATA INTO ACTION

ASCD
Alexandria, Virginia USA

ASCD®
1703 N. Beauregard St. • Alexandria, VA 22311-1714 USA
Phone: 800-933-2723 or 703-578-9600 • Fax: 703-575-5400
Website: www.ascd.org • E-mail: member@ascd.org
Author guidelines: www.ascd.org/write

Gene R. Carter, *Executive Director;* Richard Papale, *Acting Chief Program Development Officer;* Stefani Roth, *Interim Publisher;* Genny Ostertag, *Acquisitions Editor;* Julie Houtz, *Director, Book Editing & Production;* Miriam Goldstein, *Editor;* Georgia Park, *Senior Graphic Designer;* Mike Kalyan, *Production Manager;* Andrea Wilson, *Production Specialist;* Cynthia Stock, *Desktop Publisher*

ASCD Member Book No. FY14-5 (Feb. 2014, P). ASCD Member Books mail to Premium (P), Select (S), and Institutional Plus (I+) members on this schedule: Jan., PSI+; Feb., P; Apr., PSI+; May, P; July, PSI+; Aug., P; Sept., PSI+; Nov., PSI+; Dec., P. For up-to-date details on membership, see www.ascd.org/membership.

PAPERBACK ISBN: 978-1-4166-1758-7 ASCD product #114007
Also available as an e-book (see Books in Print for the ISBNs).

Quantity discounts: 10–49 copies, 10%; 50+ copies, 15%; for 1,000 or more copies, call 800-933-2723, ext. 5634, or 703-575-5634. For desk copies: www.ascd.org/deskcopy

Library of Congress Cataloging-in-Publication Data

Venables, Daniel R.
How teachers can turn data into action / Daniel R. Venables.
pages cm
Includes bibliographical references and index.
ISBN 978-1-4166-1758-7 (pbk. : alk. paper) 1. Educational indicators—United States.
2. Educational evaluation—United States. I. Title.
LB2846.V38 2014
370.72'7—dc23

2013041424

23 22 21 20 19 18 17 16 15 14 1 2 3 4 5 6 7 8 9 10 11 12 13

For my family:

Brady, Benjamin, Blue, Flo, Vinny,

Fahrney, Lucy, Cinco, and Poppy

HOW TEACHERS CAN TURN DATA INTO ACTION

Acknowledgments

This book wouldn't exist as much more than a flowchart and a few templates of my Data Action Model were it not for some key people and institutions. They all had a hand in seeing the model take manuscript form. To them, a sincere note of gratitude is in certain order.

I am grateful to the many schools that have not only field-tested this model but also embraced it with conviction and fidelity. Their results sustain my passion in sharing the model with other schools.

I offer thanks to the few pioneer schools that worked with me on early, admittedly clumsy versions of the Data Action Model: Roswell North Elementary School and Webb Bridge Middle School outside Atlanta. I may have been the one who ironed out early bugs, but these folks found them.

I express gratitude to Executive Director Lynette Guastaferro and her staff at Teaching Matters, Inc., in New York City for signing me on to be part of their pilot program implementing PLCs and the Data Action Model in six New York City schools. This opportunity has allowed me to continue to field-test, augment, and improve the model. I have appreciated and enjoyed the chance to work closely with some incredibly talented people: Dr. Naomi Cooperman, Laurie Baum, and Dr. Jennie Brotman, to mention a few. I'm surprised there is anything left of my brain after all the picking of it these people managed to do during and between my visits to New York. Teaching Matters is a top-notch organization, and it has been and continues to be a pleasure to work with.

I am grateful to my long-standing friend and colleague Cari Begin for her contributions to this work and her help in making the Data Action Model a reality in schools. She and I have worked elbow to elbow in many schools, and Cari has been a tremendous asset to me in on-site work, going to schools and training teachers to work as and lead authentic PLCs and to use the model.

I am grateful to my good friend Rob Deckert of Deckert Designs (www.deckertdesigns.com) for his talent and his patience with me regarding the work he did on the graphics related to this book and on promotional materials he does for our Grapple Institutes. Some designers are technically savvy, some are artistically savvy, but few designers are both. Rob is one of those designers.

I also wish to acknowledge Dr. Kevin Fiene, a newly acquired colleague and superintendent of East Sac County Schools in Lake View, Iowa, for his unflinching advocacy of my work. His confidence in me is almost scary.

I wish to thank two important people at ASCD whose support of this work has sustained it to completion. The first is my acquisitions editor, Genny Ostertag, who offered great feedback and insights on early drafts and has been flexible with deadlines and agreeable to my ideas about the book structure. The second person is my project manager at ASCD, Miriam Goldstein, who oversaw this work and all the various content and production components as it journeyed from draft to completed book. Her willingness to be open to my unconventional thinking is greatly appreciated.

Finally, I am grateful to my loving wife, Brady Evans, for her support of all of my pursuits, professional and personal, and this work in particular. Her belief in it never waned for a moment, even when I myself had doubts about it. For all those times I had to write by myself instead of ride (our horses) with you, and without hesitation you encouraged my *writing* when you would rather have been *riding,* I say thank you. The extent of your selflessness is beyond description. I think we shall have one or two good long rides before I share with you my great idea for a third book!

Preface

The old adage has it right: necessity really is the mother of invention. After January 2011, when my first book, *The Practice of Authentic PLCs: A Guide to Effective Teacher Teams,* was published, I found myself being asked to support teacher teams or professional learning communities (PLCs) around the United States and abroad. In that role, I have thoroughly enjoyed the challenge of helping schools at various states of readiness do the important work of authentic PLCs, and I believe that I have helped them all in some permanent, sustaining ways. But the chapter in *The Practice of Authentic PLCs* that gets the most questions (save for those pertaining to facilitating PLCs) and that has produced the most confusion for PLCs trying to implement the book's ideas is Chapter 5: "Reviewing and Responding to Data." Data are confusing. Data are messy. Data are scary. Data review is time-consuming. "We need a systematic process for looking at and responding to data" was the message I got. "And it had better be teacher-friendly. And efficient. And doable in the precious few meetings we can allocate to this and in the precious few minutes we have to do it. And it has to make a difference for our kids—and in our test scores."

Whew. Tall order, I thought. But these teachers were right: anything less was purely theoretical—good for university courses in education, but relatively useless for teachers in the trenches, doing the work as best they knew how in the scarce and coveted time they had to work with their teacher teams.

This book is the result of those requests. It was born of need and refined, streamlined, and simplified based entirely on the feedback of the teachers and teacher teams who used the Data Action Model in the trenches. The earliest versions of the model were, in retrospect, clunky and piecemeal steps of the process. Its current incarnation has the kinks worked out and provides a seamless, integrated process for going from initial views of data to real-life action in the classroom based on the data.

Most of the chapters in this book end with a section titled "From the Trenches," which illustrates main concepts using realistic school vignettes. The demographics of the schools in these vignettes range from elementary to high school, small schools to large schools, urban schools to rural schools, and affluent schools to Title I schools. It is my hope that through these vignettes, readers from a wide range of educational experiences will appreciate the real-world applicability of the Data Action Model.

Daniel R. Venables
Driftwood Farm
Gilbert, South Carolina
June 2013

Introduction

Why Is (Working with) Data So Hard?

In my 30-plus years as an educator, I have realized that many teachers and administrators find looking at and making sense of data an unpleasant task for many reasons. Some find it just too intimidating to plow through table upon table of numbers and try to make sense of them. Others have an unspoken but underlying belief that data do not *really* tell them anything important.

Others experience a painful flashback to the math and statistics courses with which they struggled in college. And for others—arguably, most—there isn't enough time in their busy workday to submerge themselves in graphs, tables, and charts to produce what they think will be, in the end, facts about their students' learning that they already knew or at least suspected. Add to this the fact that for other, more seasoned teachers, reviewing data was not done for many years in education, so their prevailing attitude is "We got by just fine without it."

Of course, in our post–No Child Left Behind (NCLB) and present Common Core State Standards (CCSS) era, we know differently. We know that to *not* review state and CCSS data is to put our students at certain, even measurable, disadvantage. Data aren't everything, to be sure, but they represent the best, most reliable way to see where students currently are in their learning and to identify instructional actions to get them to where we would like them to be. If we don't use data to do so, we are left to rely on our *hunches* for making important instructional decisions. As we'll see, hunches are sometimes wrong. Even if our hunches are wrong only 25 percent of the time, that's still a lot of time to spend trying to fix problems that may only be symptoms of greater, more encompassing issues that may well go undetected. That's time we don't have. Educators are experiencing an increasing sense of urgency to fix problems related to student achievement and can't afford to misdiagnose students' learning gaps. Now more than ever, we need to be right in what we believe those gaps are and in what we believe their root causes are. A careful look at quality, relevant data can help us achieve this goal.

In helping schools review and respond to their data, I have seen a tendency for administrators to provide year-end data to teachers and let teachers decide what to do with it. This approach often results in teachers and teacher teams giving the data a cursory look, with no intent to use the data to make instructional changes. This pattern does not reflect teacher disinterest in improving student achievement as much as it does their general discomfort with turning numbers into action.

This feeling has partly to do with the size and kind of data teachers are often asked to review. For example, large *macrodata,* such as end-of-course test data, seldom produce specific, nuanced instructional changes. In the absence of more detailed *microdata,* teachers respond to large data with an equally broad brush: "We can see our students with disabilities are sorely lacking in proficiency," or "Once again, our girls have outperformed our boys in reading comprehension." Little useful information is gleaned by taking such a cursory look at the data; therefore, teachers will revert to the status quo, and no real instructional change is likely to result. It's not that teachers *resist* changing instructional practice (although some do), but more that, in many cases, the data are revealing things the teachers already knew.

The problem lies in viewing only the macrodata and stopping there. It turns out that the kinds of information that can provide the impetus for real change lie in the details—the microdata. A good place to start, macrodata may tell us *what* is happening and perhaps even *to whom* it is happening, but to find out *why* it is happening and *how* to fix it, teachers and teacher teams need to turn to the more detailed and frequent microdata. To help review and implement this sort of data, I have developed the Data Action Model.

Data Action Model at a Glance

The Data Action Model is a systematic process for reviewing and responding to data. I have already noted that teachers are generally good at *looking at* data; the extent to which that review translates into changes in the classroom is quite a different matter. The Data Action Model helps. It begins with a structured look at the macrodata and then drills down into the smaller microdata, often bringing in additional relevant data to fully understand the root causes of any learning gaps that are uncovered. Then learning gaps are linked to corresponding instructional gaps, and the process culminates with a goal-driven action plan, complete with a metric for assessing the effectiveness of the plan once implemented.

The Data Action Model is composed of three main phases: Gathering and Reviewing Data, Identifying Gaps, and Planning for and Evaluating Action (see Figure 1). Each of these phases is incorporated into five data meetings. Each data meeting is broken down into manageable steps for teacher teams to follow. The process is cyclic in nature; once a team has met its data-driven goal at the end of one cycle, the team begins anew and explores new data (or returns to the original data set) to uncover other learning and instructional gaps needing remedy.

One cycle of the Data Action Model normally requires five separate hour-long meetings from start to finish. Depending on the nature of the data used in the first meeting, this meeting time might be shorter. The Data Action Model normally spans approximately nine weeks (one grading period) if the meetings are held weekly. This is because there is a four-week Implementation Period between Data Meeting 4 and Data Meeting 5 (see Figure 2).

It should be pointed out that the data meeting template in Figure 2 presupposes that the data initially reviewed by the PLC are broad data, as in end-of-course or Common Core assessment data. These data are most likely reviewed in August or September, at the start of the school year. However, teacher teams will revisit this template once the year has begun (but before new macrodata such as Common Core assessment data are in); in this case, most PLCs are reviewing district benchmark data, teacher-designed

— Figure 1 —

Data Action Model

Schedule of Data Meetings Using Data on Taught Topics

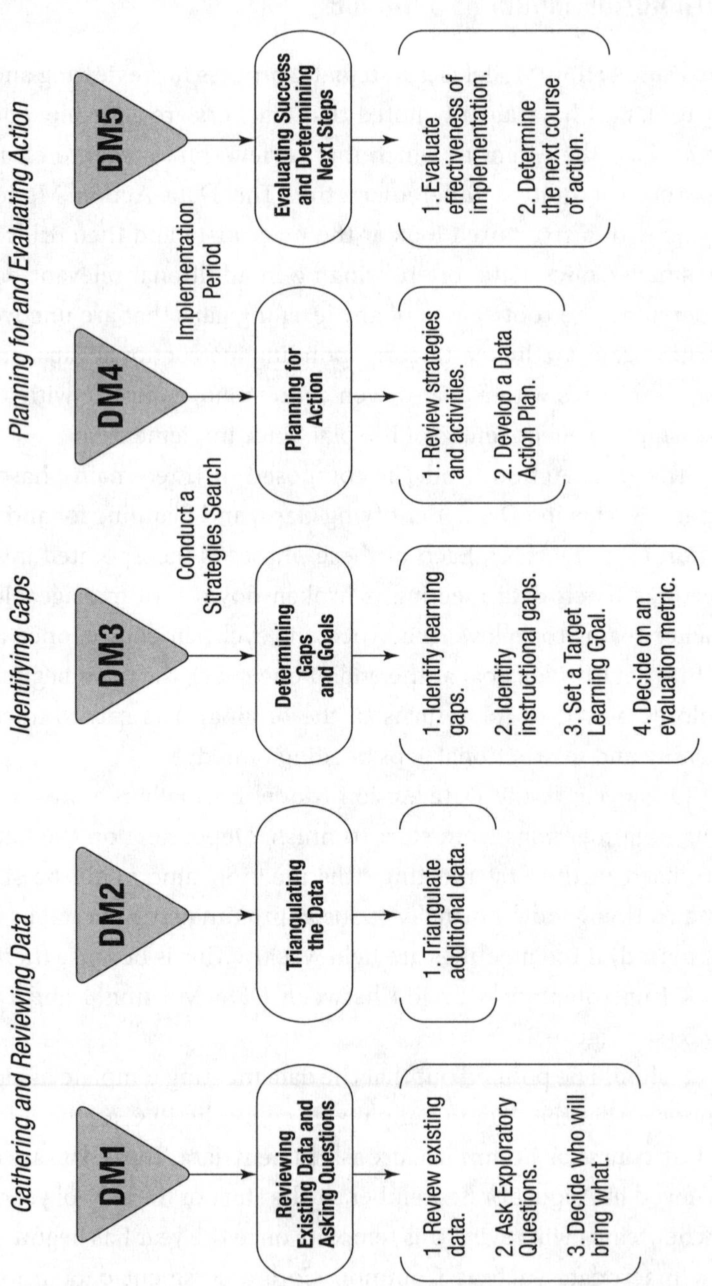

— Figure 2 —

Schedule of Meetings Using Data on Taught Topics

Meeting	Focus	What to Do (and in what order)
Data Meeting 1	Reviewing existing data and asking questions	1. Review existing data. 2. Ask Exploratory Questions. 3. Decide who will bring what.
Data Meeting 2	Triangulating the data	1. Triangulate additional data.
Data Meeting 3	Determining gaps and goals	1. Identify learning gaps. 2. Identify instructional gaps. 3. Set a Target Learning Goal. 4. Decide on an evaluation metric.
Data Meeting 4	Planning for action	Conduct a Strategies Search; then 1. Review strategies and activities. 2. Develop a Data Action Plan.
PLC Meetings 1–4	Implementation period (four weeks)	Look at student and teacher work; troubleshoot obstacles; look at texts, research.
Data Meeting 5	Evaluating success and determining next steps	1. Evaluate effectiveness of implementation. 2. Determine the next course of action.

assessment data, or pre-test data on an upcoming unit they are planning. With pre-test data or data derived from diagnostic assessments of untaught material, the cycle of meetings varies, as shown in Figure 3 (also see "Using backward-looking data" and "Using forward-looking data" in Data Meeting 5, and Figure 12 on page 111).

Note that when teams begin with pre-test data on a unit they are preparing to teach, the cycle is shortened considerably. Most units are approximately two weeks from pre-test to post-test. That means the full data cycle is at most four weeks, often shorter. It also means that teams should allow ample time between gathering pre-test data and teaching the unit so that they have time to decide on instructional strategies before actually teaching the unit. Otherwise, teams tend to rush straight from identifying gaps to teaching standards the way they have always taught them, without regard

— Figure 3 —

Schedule of Meetings Using Data on Untaught Topics		
Meeting	**Focus**	**What to Do** (and in what order)
Data Meeting 1	Reviewing pre-test data and identifying learning gaps	1. Review pre-test data. 2. Identify learning gaps. 3. Set a Target Learning Goal.
Data Meeting 2	Planning for action	Conduct a Strategies Search; then 1. Review strategies and activities. 2. Develop a Data Action Plan. 3. Decide on an evaluation metric.
PLC Meetings 1 and 2	Implementation period (two weeks)	Look at student and teacher work; troubleshoot obstacles; look at texts, research.
Data Meeting 3	Evaluating success and determining next steps	1. Evaluate effectiveness of implementation using post-test data. 2. Determine the next course of action.

for what might actually be the best way to teach those standards. The result, too often, is that no actual instructional change occurs.

The Necessity and Pitfalls of Cycles

More than once, I have referred to the notion of cycles. Although the length of the cycles varies considerably—as in the case of the cycles depicted in Figures 2 and 3—the Data Action Model is necessarily cyclic in nature. Data are reviewed, gaps are identified, goals are set, and action plans are implemented, and that cycle is repeated as new data are reviewed, new gaps are identified, and so on. This is to be expected.

That said, it is also somewhat restrictive to think only in terms of cycles. The danger is that teacher teams will try to pigeonhole cycles into fixed time frames that, in reality, may or may not be applicable to the content targeted in any one cycle. Cycles vary in length and must remain flexible if they are to be useful. Teams should be aware of this point as they map out their cycles.

A Note About This Book

Initially, I organized this book by chapters that each described a step in the Data Action Model. However, teacher teams who actually used the model were more interested in what should be happening at each *meeting*—not at each *step*. They were spot-on. If the Data Action Model is to be truly useful to teams trying in earnest to follow it, it should not be organized by steps but, rather, by meetings.

Based on this important feedback, I completely reorganized the contents of this book to be set up primarily by meetings as opposed to steps. The result is more PLC-friendly, as it delineates what should be accomplished at each PLC meeting. Data Meeting 1, then, is the first chapter; Data Meeting 2, the second; and so forth.

Throughout this book, I use the terms *PLC* and *teacher team* to refer to the same thing. While I acknowledge that the term *PLC* encompasses some characteristics that may or may not be present in all teacher teams, for our purpose here, I use the two terms interchangeably. The same is true for my use of the terms *PLC coach* and *PLC facilitator*, both of which I use to refer to the teacher who leads the teacher team. Finally, I often refer to the Common Core State Standards (CCSS) simply as the *Common Core,* as they tend to be called in most education circles these days.

In the chapters that follow, we will explore these phases in detail and illustrate implementation of each one with vignettes of schools that are using the model. (All vignettes are fictional, describing schools that are composites of actual schools, and all names used are fictional.) Before we turn to what should happen during Data Meeting 1, it is important to be clear about what we mean by data, where we find them, what types exist, and how those can be used to improve teacher and student performance.

Before Meeting

Developing Data Literacy

Why Data?

The mathematicians at Google can predict the start and severity of the flu season before the Centers for Disease Control and Prevention (CDC) can. Moreover, they can predict where the big outbreaks will be and where the flu will "move" next. How? By examining the data from flu-related searches (e.g., for flu symptoms or treatments), Google can track the path of the flu before the CDC has records of it (Mayer-Schönberger & Cukier, 2013). The reason is that people generally search the Internet for information about the flu at its onset, and only after their symptoms are sufficiently severe do they see their doctor, who then records the information, by law, for the CDC. In this way, Google is ahead of the curve—figuratively and literally—in what it knows about the upcoming flu season: the graph of the frequency of flu-related searches aligns perfectly with and precedes the CDC's graph of actual flu cases (Dukic, Lopes, & Polson, 2009). In the absence of these powerful and predictive data, Google and the CDC might be left with only their hunches about where the flu would strike next or how severe it would be.

Let's suppose you were offered $1 million to unlock a stranger's cell phone in only three tries. The lock on the cell phone is the familiar 3 × 3 dot-grid pattern lock. Without any other information, you would have no clue what the unlocking pattern would be and almost certainly would fail to unlock it in only three tries. But imagine you were also given a rank-ordered list of the 25 most common lock patterns from a survey of 200 cell phone users. What would you do? I suspect most people would try the top three patterns listed in hopes of cracking the code. There's no guarantee that this would work, but it would offer your best chance of success. Without it, you'd be left with only unsubstantiated hunches.

A Word About Hunches

As mentioned in this book's Introduction, if we don't use data to inform our instructional decisions, we're often left doing things based on hunches. Although hunches are sometimes right, they are sometimes wrong, too—which can lead to actions that may only treat a symptom of a greater underlying cause as to why our students (or a subpopulation of our students) are not performing as well as we would like. To get a more informed and complete view and one that has the highest chance of being accurate—as in our cell phone experiment—we need to look at the data.

One of the principal assets of the Data Action Model is that it slows down the process that comes between looking at data and reacting to the data. When teachers and teacher teams rush to make decisions about what students need without having looked carefully at the data, they are often attempting to address a challenge that may not actually be a root cause of the broader problem (Love, 2009). By slowing down the decision-making process, the Data Action Model helps teachers and teacher teams more closely and more accurately diagnose where their students are and what they should do as a result.

That said, I feel compelled to offer a thought or two regarding the role of hunches. Most teachers know where their students are lacking. Even teachers with just a few years of experience can speculate on what content will be most difficult, which areas will demand extra time, and which areas will likely need repeated assessment and intervention. This is to be expected. In the absence of hard data, teacher teams can speculate about where their students' learning gaps are, and these speculations can begin the process of using data to improve instruction. But these hunches are merely a starting point—the doorway leading into the Data Action Model's sequence of steps. To proceed as though our hunches were more than a starting point and immediately jump into action is a risky proposition. What if we have it wrong? What if what we posit as a cause turns out to be a symptom of another (undiagnosed) cause? By thoroughly examining the data—all relevant data—we just about eliminate the possibility of committing this time- and energy-consuming error.

Data as a Snapshot

It is important to bear in mind that information revealed by student achievement data represents a particular level of mastery at a particular time. Therefore, it is a mere snapshot of where a student is at any one time. After all, if it were the final call of information about a student's mastery, we really wouldn't have a reason to do much with it. There would be no need to analyze it and use it to formulate a plan for instructional changes. The fact that student data offer a temporal snapshot is what makes this information useful.

Data Teams and Professional Learning Communities

Authentic professional learning communities (PLCs) regularly review and respond to grade-level or subject-specific data (Venables, 2011). Sometimes the data pertain to an individual teacher, and the instructional recommendations are made *by* individual teachers *for* individual teachers. Most often, however, the PLC examines data collectively to identify trends in students' learning. This approach leads to improvement not only of individual teachers but also of whole departments (Vescio, Ross, & Adams, 2008).

Some schools, even those with established, well-functioning PLCs, assemble a team of teachers whose job is to look at data from each subject or grade level. These data teams—or inquiry teams, as some schools call them—provide each department or grade level with a summary of their findings about student achievement in that subject or grade level. The school's own individual PLCs then set goals and make instructional changes based on the data team's findings. There are some advantages to having data teams external to individual PLCs—for example, in providing a consistent review and analysis of data across departments. Nonetheless, I suggest that this practice is counterproductive. When data review is limited to a team of teachers outside the PLC, the teachers *within* the PLC will likely not spend much time reviewing their own data and consequently will have a less clear understanding of their students' learning gaps. Although the external data team approach has worked in some schools, I have witnessed it becoming less popular as increasingly more schools now ask their departmental or grade-level PLCs to analyze their own data.

I believe that the teachers who own the data ought to be the teachers who review the data. My advice is to scrap external data teams and instead train all members of PLCs to become comfortable with and proficient at reviewing their own data and creating their own action plans. In this way, teacher teams make sense of their data together, and the conclusions they draw about where students are lacking and what to do about it are collaborative decisions that generally foster greater buy-in by all members of the PLC. When teacher teams own the review of the data, they also own the response to those data that, in the end, they must implement at the classroom level (Reeves, 2004).

Formative and Summative Data

Before 2001, when No Child Left Behind (NCLB) legislation passed, educators outside of college and university courses didn't talk a lot about formative and summative assessments and data. Since then, these terms have garnered a great deal of attention, yet they can remain confusing for some teachers. Let me attempt to make the distinction clear.

Formative data are used to *inform* instruction. Formative data provide information about how students are doing during instruction so that actions—or, more specifically, reactions—can occur to modify instruction based on that information. Formative use of data enables teachers to improve instruction before it's too late. Formative assessments can be as large and encompassing as a quarterly exam covering multiple chapters or as small as a single "check for understanding" question a teacher asks the class after presenting new material. In both examples, the information gleaned from the assessment is meant solely to assess where students are *at that particular point in time* so that the teacher can address student gaps in learning and adjust instruction accordingly.

Summative data are used to *evaluate* instruction. Summative data exist to classify, categorize, and label students' level of mastery and, as such, to classify, categorize, and label the teacher's accompanying instruction. Summative data are "dead end" data, typically gathered at the end of instruction with no pretense of affecting instruction. PARCC and Smarter Balanced assessment data and state end-of-course data are almost always summative data. When the U.S. Department of Agriculture labels beef with its USDA grade, that information is summative. The label is final. There is no expectation that the classification will change.

Rick Stiggins (2001) makes a helpful distinction between formative and summative assessments: formative assessments are assessments *for* learning, while summative assessments are assessments *of* learning. In other words, formative assessment data affect learning that *is happening,* whereas summative assessment data label learning that *has happened.* An apt analogy points out that formative assessment is to summative assessment as a yearly physical is to an autopsy. Both the physical and the autopsy involve medical assessment. Both provide data. But the physical provides information that can still effect changes in the patient's health, whereas the autopsy simply provides information after the fact, with no implication or intention of changing or improving the patient's health.

In contrasting these types of data, how the data are *used* is the real litmus test determining whether they are formative or summative. If data do not lead to adjustments in instruction—regardless of how big or small the data are—then the effect essentially is that of summative data. If the results of a teacher-designed quiz don't inform the teacher's instruction regarding what students know and do not know and what the teacher will do about the gaps observed, then the quiz might just as well have occurred at the end of the year, along with other, larger summative assessments. The determining factor is *how the data are used* (Brookhart, 2009; Venables, 2011).

Let's revisit the example that opened this chapter. The data from the CDC documenting cases of the flu are largely after the fact and therefore act as summative data. Google search data on flu symptoms, in contrast, precede full-blown cases of the flu and serve more as formative data insofar as there is still time for intervention that could affect the extent of an outbreak. A key aspect of formative data lies in the data's ability to be predictive. Indeed, one of the most common sources of formative data is the pre-test, given before a new unit of instruction to determine what students already know.

Sources of Data

If there is any myth that ought to be dispelled in a book on data, it is the notion that data are limited to "big" data—results from CCSS assessments, end-of-course tests and projects, the final exam, or the district's quarterly report. These big data sources get all the press, so to speak, and for good reason: the end-of-year test data (whether CCSS or state assessment data) serve as the most widely used metric for how our students—and we teachers—did all year. It is the scale that weighs the fruits of our labor. But these sources provide generally summative data and do little to improve instruction—at least not alone.

End-of-year data, whether from state or CCSS assessments, provide general information about student mastery of standards across subgroups and indicate overarching trends in student performance. Individual skills mastered (or not) by individual students are less apparent, and almost nothing about the specific instruction that led to students' performance can be learned by examining such expansive, cumulative data. For that level of understanding, we need to look at smaller data (Boudett, City, & Murnane, 2005; Curtis & City, 2009). Specific information about where students failed to master skills and lack understanding resides in the multiple points of data embedded in the instruction, the planning of the instruction, the assessments, and the student work that led up to the year-end summative assessment. It is here where we spend most of our time in reviewing data; the broad strokes painted by year-end data are merely reasonable starting points.

Consider a sports analogy: can you imagine a high school football coach trying to improve his players' performance of the plays used in Friday night's game if the only data he had told him whether or not his team won the game? It is the smaller data that emerge along the way, during the game, that become useful.

In addition, data's usefulness in informing classroom instruction varies according to the *frequency* of data collection (Stiggins, 2001; Venables, 2011). Year-end data gathered once annually, although important, tend to be less useful in changing classroom practice than weekly teacher-administered quizzes that cover the content taught that week. My experience has led me to believe that the bigger the data, the less direct their effect typically is on instructional change. The *microdata* are often more useful than the *macrodata* in improving teaching and learning (Stiggins, 2001; Venables, 2011).

For example, daily warm-ups, when done well, can be a tremendous source of formative data for the teacher who uses the results of the warm-ups to guide and pace instruction. Every time a teacher asks a question of students—regardless of their responses—the teacher learns something useful about what students know and understand or what they do not. Such microdata should not be overlooked: they are an important source of information that enable teachers to adjust instruction and align it to students' needs *even as instruction is occurring.*

I like to call this approach *bat teaching.* Bats locate their prey (most often mosquitoes, which is why I welcome bats on my farm) not by seeing it, but by sending out a vocal signal and judging the prey's location by the audio signal that bounces back. Based on that return signal, bats adjust their movement and close in on the prey. Frequency is key here: how successful would a bat be in locating its prey if it only occasionally sent out a couple of big audio signals? No doubt, the bat would starve.

Just as bats pursue their prey by echolocation, effective teachers continually send out signals to see where their students' understandings are and, based on students' return signals, adjust their instruction to close in on their students' level of understanding. Virtually everything a teacher does in the classroom can provide information about where students are in their mastery of any given topic. Student responses—whether given to questions asked during instruction, offered during a warm-up activity, or recorded on individual whiteboards—are valuable sources of formative data that help the classroom teacher decide what to do next and how best to do it. And just as with the bat's search for prey, frequency is key here: the frequency with which data are collected is instrumental in making those small changes in instruction that add up to big changes in student learning and achievement.

Specific examples of sources of macrodata and microdata include the following:

Sources of Macrodata

- Student scores on end-of-course/CCSS assessments
- Student scores on common formative assessments
- Student grades on projects
- Student scores on district assessments
- Student scores on PSAT, SAT, and ACT
- Student scores on Advanced Placement (AP) exams
- Student scores on DIBELS
- Student scores on subject placement exams
- Student scores on computer-based modules
- Student scores on unit pre-tests

Sources of Microdata

- Student performance on quizzes
- Student responses to teacher questions during lessons
- Student questions during lessons
- Student performance on warm-up questions
- Student responses to ticket-out-the-door questions
- Student performance during guided practice
- Student performance during group work
- Student performance during independent practice
- Student performance on homework assignments
- Student responses to checks for understanding
- Student explanations at the board
- Student posters
- Student notebooks
- Student portfolios
- Student reflections in journals
- Student performance on writing assignments

Small Data for Big Questions

Macrodata, such as end-of-course or CCSS assessment data, are particularly well suited for providing teacher teams with the information necessary to ask big questions about their students' learning (Boudett & Steele, 2007), like *Why are our African American females outperforming our African American males in both math and language arts?* or *Why are our students performing less well in algebra skills than other students in similar schools in our county?* These are valid questions that a teacher team might raise when looking at the big data. In fact, in the next chapter, we will formalize this whole notion of asking questions from the big data as we define and examine *Exploratory Questions*. To be sure, these questions drive further investigation by the PLC.

It is the smaller data, however, that provide the information necessary to *answer* the bigger questions raised by the big data. As Boudett, City, and Murnane (2005) point out, "It is important to examine a wide range of data, not just results on standardized tests. Indeed, . . . an analysis of standardized test results raises more questions than it answers. Examining other types of evidence on students' skills and knowledge is needed to answer these questions" (p. 6).

In all cases, our ultimate purpose in reviewing and responding to data is to improve some aspect of our students' learning. Note the orientation here: our aim is less focused on improving some aspect of our *teaching* and more directly targeted on some aspect of our students' *learning*. This process necessarily begins with asking the right questions. But asking good questions is not an end in itself. It is only when we gather enough microdata—the smaller pieces of relevant information—and begin viewing and analyzing these data that a clearer picture of our students' learning emerges. Then we have enough information to respond to the big questions.

Data Inventory

Schools and teachers are bombarded by data. This was not always the case; when I began my teaching career in 1980, there were a few standardized tests, such as the SAT and the PSAT, AP exams, and developmental reading tests for elementary students, but very little was done with them in terms of informing instruction. After the NCLB Act of 2001, states produced end-of-year assessments; schools and districts produced quarterly, interim, and benchmark assessments; and all of those assessments produced lots of data. In addition, the data were organized, packaged, and reported in many different ways. Tables upon tables and charts upon graphs dizzied more than a few principals and teachers trying to glean information from them. It wasn't a bad thing for teachers to review these data reports, but the analysis was simply overwhelming for teachers who didn't have the requisite skills in detailed data analysis.

More than a decade after NCLB and its resultant data surge, most teachers still feel just as overwhelmed with these data reports. As DuFour, DuFour, Eaker, and Many (2006) have said, schools are "data rich and information poor" (p. 215). Although these NCLB-related data are mostly considered macrodata—and therefore useful starting points—teacher teams are left with the daunting task of having to decide which data reports are most useful and should be investigated further. This task presents a challenge to PLCs: how do busy teacher teams decide what to spend precious planning time looking at? But decide they must, which is why it is essential that teams begin by taking inventory of the types of data to which they have access—typically, PARCC, Smarter Balanced, state, district, and school-level data.

Before gathering relevant microdata, we must do two things. First, we must in a structured way review existing data—most likely, the available macrodata—and do so thoroughly enough that we're able to do the second task effectively, which is to ask Exploratory Questions. We'll examine these two important tasks in Data Meeting 1.

Data Meeting 1

Reviewing Existing Data and Asking Questions

NOTICE

WONDER

ASK

BRING

TRACK

IDENTIFY

SET

SEARCH

DEVELOP

IMPLEMENT

EVALUATE

A Word About Protocols

Protocols are tools. Tools make the job at hand easier to do. Protocols help teachers keep their discussions focused, their time used efficiently, and their actions purposeful and impactful. They keep us on track so that we talk about the stuff that matters and do so in a structured, safe way that promotes depth and honesty of discourse. They are useful in a wide range of educational settings, from looking at student work, to setting group norms, to troubleshooting obstacles. To learn more about using protocols in these and other settings, see *The Practice of Authentic PLCs: A Guide to Effective Teacher Teams* (Venables, 2011); *The Power of Protocols: An Educator's Guide to Better Practice* (McDonald, Mohr, Dichter, & McDonald, 2007); and *Protocols for Professional Learning* (Easton, 2009).

For our purposes here, protocols are useful for looking at data and discussing how best to respond to the data. In addition to providing structure and keeping us focused, they also take the stinger out of the oft-threatening task of looking at data—particularly for the scores of teachers who, by their own admission, would prefer to have nothing to do with data. I affectionately refer to these folks as "dataphobes," and I spend a fair amount of time with teacher teams helping them get past the initial dread of reviewing charts, tables, and graphs. The fact that teachers most often view data publicly, as a team, doesn't help dataphobes' feelings of numerical inadequacy. Protocols can come to the rescue.

One protocol we use in the Data Action Model, the *Notice and Wonder Protocol,* helps take the angst out of the prospect of facing data. It also helps teachers and teacher teams who are examining data in three ways:

1. It makes it easier for teachers to internalize and make sense of the data;
2. It forces teachers to have a conversation about what the data actually say; and
3. It assuages the temptation on the parts of teachers to rush to conclusions prematurely.

Let's take a closer look, beginning with a cautionary comment on the dangers of jumping to (often erroneous) conclusions.

Do First: Review Existing Data

After teacher teams have inventoried their existing data as described in the "Before Meeting" chapter, it's time for the teams to choose one or two data reports from the usual mass of reports and to begin the cycle of data inquiry. In most cases, this will be macrodata and, most often, state or CCSS assessment data or district-administered quarterly assessment data. Regardless of the data's specific source and composition, the information chosen in this first step typically paints in broad brushstrokes where students are in their mastery, and here is where we rightfully begin. As we'll see as we continue through each step of the Data Action Model, there will be sufficient time later to paint in very fine brush lines.

The Problem That Isn't

The Data Action Model is designed so that teachers and teacher teams engage thoroughly with their data before deciding what the problems of learning and practice are. Indeed, the first phase, Gathering and Reviewing Data, makes up a full third of the model, yet it includes nary a mention of teams attempting to elucidate problems of student learning that are present in the data. This, of course, is an eventual goal of the model, but it will not be addressed in significant detail until Data Meeting 3: Determining Gaps and Goals.

There is a good reason for this delay in identifying problem areas. In my consulting practice, prior to developing the Data Action Model, I kept seeing a consistent and problematic phenomenon crop up with even the most well-intentioned data teams and PLCs: in their zeal to improve student achievement, these teams rushed to find "the problem" from the data. They would come to the meeting room with a hunch as to what the problems were in their students' learning and thus reviewed the data only cursorily—if at all—and used it chiefly to corroborate what they already believed to be true about their students' weaknesses. By viewing the data only through the lens of a preconceived problem, they saw only the numbers that supported their preconceived expectations and often overlooked other areas in need of attention—even dire attention. Sometimes, their hunches *were* dead-on, and the data did indeed support their hunches about their students' learning gaps. Other times, however—very often, in fact—teams focused on an area that was relatively small in comparison to what I started calling their other "bleeding arteries." In other words, their area of focus was not the central problem but instead symptomatic of a different, often broader problem. At best, this misaligned focus led to a Band-Aid approach to solving their real problem; at worst, it left them spending untold energy and time solving "the problem that isn't." If the problem is misdiagnosed, after all, the solution cannot be effective.

A few years back, I was assisting a 9th grade Algebra I PLC whose members, after briefly reviewing the results of a district-administered quarterly assessment, decided that their students couldn't successfully solve word problems that required them to apply their knowledge of two-step equations. These teachers' knee-jerk assessment of the problem was that they weren't giving the students enough practice in solving word problems with two-step equations and that the solution was, therefore, to provide the students with more opportunities to practice such problems. Only after delving into the data in more detail and with additional sources did the team realize that the students' deficiencies did not result from practicing too few word problems involving two-step equations; rather, the word problems they *did* practice were all essentially clones of only three different word problems. The students had become proficient at solving those three problems, but they never understood the underlying concepts behind the application of two-step equations. Their lack of understanding showed up on the district assessment when they had to solve problems that didn't resemble any of the three problems they had "learned."

Time and again, I witnessed this same phenomenon as I worked with various teams in a host of different schools. What was needed, I decided, was a protocol that forced both a thorough look at the data *and* a delay in concluding where the problems were, why they existed, and how they could be solved. The result was the creation of the Notice and Wonder Protocol.

Notice and Wonder Protocol

This protocol is remarkably popular wherever I share it. Teachers appreciate that the Notice and Wonder Protocol is a simple and effective tool that offers a nonthreatening way for them to view data and share observations about what they see. Anyone can *notice* and anyone can *wonder,* right? The details of the protocol appear in the Appendix (pp. 114–115).

Here's an overview of how the protocol works. Teachers are given a data report (or two) of some kind and quietly and individually review it. In Round 1, on an index card or in their notebooks, they record several factual things they notice in the data. These observations are free of inference and shared without discussion; teams often post their statements in a shared Google document. In Round 2, on the back of the index card, they note "wonders": *wonder whys*, *wonder ifs*, *wonder whethers*, and *wonder hows*. These observations may not be outright inferences but usually contain a speculative implication. Teachers share these within the group while a volunteer scribes them on chart paper. No discussion occurs at this time, except for follow-up questions the team facilitator may ask of the teacher or the team. These, too, are posted for the team to see.

To look at the Notice and Wonder Protocol in action, consider the table in Figure 4. This report reflects how each subgroup of 7th grade English language arts (ELA) students performed across five strands on a midyear standardized assessment. The subgroups are based on gender, race, economic status, students with disabilities, and English language learners.

— Figure 4 —

7th Grade ELA Midyear Assessment Report									
District		Teacher	All			Reading Tracker Subgroup by Strand			
School		Grade	7						
Date		Subject	ELA			Assessment Date 3-Feb-12 FORM G No. of Students 123			
Percentage of Items Answered Correctly									
Subgroup	**Mean**	**Gathering Information Skills**		**Organizing Information Skills**		**Analyzing Information Skills**		**Linking Information Skills**	
No. of Students	**Scaled Score**	**Literal Level**		**Interpretive Level**		**Analytical Level**		**Critical Level**	
All Students (123)	757	70		58		73		80	
Female (65)	760	73	11/15	71	5/7	78	7/9	80	4/5
Male (58)	754	67	10/15	43	3/7	67	6/9	80	4/5
White (47)	772	73	11/15	100	7/7	78	7/9	100	5/5
Black (32)	730	60	9/15	57	4/7	33	3/9	40	2/5
Asian (6)	812	100	15/15	100	7/7	89	8/9	80	4/5
Hispanic (26)	726	33	5/15	43	3/7	56	5/9	80	4/5
Multiracial (12)	743	80	12/15	29	2/7	44	4/9	80	4/5
ED (49)	728	53	8/15	57	4/7	33	3/9	40	2/5
SWD (22)	702	27	4/15	43	3/7	22	2/9	40	2/5
ELL (18)	712	27	4/15	14	1/7	67	6/9	40	2/5

Note: ED = economically disadvantaged; SWD = students with disabilities; ELL = English language learners.

The percentages listed in the table represent the mean percentage of test items the student subgroup answered correctly in each particular strand. For example, the first subgroup, representing the 65 female students tested, had a mean scaled score of 760 and, on average, correctly answered 73 percent (11 of 15) of the questions in the Gathering Information Skills strand, 71 percent (5 of 7) of the questions in the Organizing Information Skills strand, 78 percent (7 of 9) of the questions in the Analyzing Information Skills strand, and 80 percent (4 of 5) of the questions in the Linking Information strand. (Note that the percentages are based on the average number of questions answered correctly and have been rounded up if their actual value is a decimal greater than or equal to 0.5. For example, a mean percentage listed as 100 percent may actually have been a mean of 4.5 questions answered correctly and then rounded to 5 of 5.)

The teacher team reviewing these data, the ELA 7 PLC, includes five ELA classroom teachers and one special education teacher who works with each of the classroom teachers on a rotating basis, assisting the 22 students with disabilities who are in general education classes. The ELA 7 PLC meets twice weekly during their hour-long common planning period, and one of those meetings is strictly dedicated to looking at and responding to data. Their PLC coach (facilitator) begins the meeting by projecting on the interactive whiteboard the data table in Figure 4.

For this data set, teachers in the ELA 7 PLC might offer the following *Notice Statements* in Round 1:

- I notice that more female students were tested than male students.
- I notice that, overall, students answered at least 70 percent of the test items correctly in three of the four strands.
- I notice that students, on average, scored least well in the Organizing/Interpretive strand.
- I notice that Hispanic students did least well in comparison with other subgroups in the Gathering/Literal strand.

The Notice Statements that are shared may be superficial in nature, as with the first one listed here, or they may pivot on some real and significant facts about the performance of a student subgroup, such as the third and fourth statements listed. All of the statements made are factual, as the protocol instructs, and it does not matter at this point that some of the Notice Statements are meatier than others. What's more important at this juncture is that all members of the team—even the dataphobes—have offered Notice Statements.

By having to make only factual observations, according to the protocol, the team is freed up from the common, self-imposed responsibility to draw conclusions and rush to try to fix problems. Instead, the team can look at simply what the data are saying. Their focus is entirely on the *what* and not on the *why* or *how to fix it.* This step is liberating for teachers who are uncomfortable with the notion of looking at data in the first place and who are used to dealing with the tacit expectation that they must quickly determine solutions. Because the protocol does not allow proposed solutions or even mention of underlying problems and asks teachers only to discuss what is revealed by the data in a factual, objective way, teachers who usually prefer to hang back during data conversations tend to feel more comfortable contributing.

Afterward, in Round 2, teacher teams are given the green light to make speculations and deeper observations in the context of *Wonder Statements.* For the ELA data in Figure 4, the ELA 7 PLC might offer the following Wonder Statements:

- I wonder why students did better in higher-order strands (Analytical and Critical Levels) than on the Literal and Interpretive Levels.
- I wonder why our female students are doing so much better on the Organizing/Interpretive level than their male counterparts.
- I wonder what percentage of our students of color (black, Asian, Hispanic, multiracial) are eligible for free or reduced lunch.
- I wonder if our expectations of our students in the Interpretive Level are too high or too low during instruction.

Without making a conscious effort to push the conversation to a deeper level, the transition from Round 1 (notice) to Round 2 (wonder) naturally does just that. There is good reason for this transition. *Notice Statements* focus on what happened, whereas *Wonder Statements* congregate around why it happened, how it happened, and what might be possible.

A couple of points are in order on Notice and Wonder Statements. First, the Notice Statements shared in Round 1 often resurface in Round 2 as Wonder Statements. For example, referring back to our ELA 7 data, a teacher might offer the Notice Statement *I notice that African American students had greatest difficulty with the Analytical items, while Hispanic students had greatest difficulty at the Literal Level.* In Round 2, a different teacher (or possibly the same teacher) might share the Wonder Statement *I wonder how we're teaching analyzing skills that our black students do so poorly on this strand.* Although Wonder Statements might reflect earlier Notice Statements, it is important for teams to realize that this isn't necessary; all Wonder Statements are fair game whether or not they are connected to previous Notice Statements.

Second, by the end of Round 2, the team has probably listed 15 or 20 Wonder Statements. As the team keeps its focus on its eventual goal of improving instruction, members inevitably realize that not all Wonder Statements are of equal value in terms of advancing that goal. Some of the Wonder Statements may even seem relatively insignificant compared with others. For example, *I wonder how much higher these kids would score if they read more at home* is less valuable to the team than *I wonder if we're spending too much time with the vocabulary quizzes.* In other cases, some Wonder Statements on the list can be answered with just a bit of checking, such as *I wonder how many days we spent on improper fractions* or *I wonder if the students with special needs are permitted to use a calculator on the decimals module.* Although these are all legitimate Wonder Statements, they do not stand out to the team as areas that warrant further pursuit using the Data Action Model. During this step in the model, team members simply discuss the Wonder Statements posted in the list. Are there areas that are mentioned several times? Do several statements fall under one umbrella topic? Can the list be collapsed into a handful of categories? Are there any "bleeding arteries"? Which statements stand to lead to the most impactful action?

At the conclusion of the Notice and Wonder Protocol, teacher teams will have explored the data and internalized what the data have revealed, and they are well on their way to thinking about what is going on in their students' learning and where the problems may lie. Again, they are not solving any of the problems just yet—indeed, they have only begun to identify them—they are simply making sense of what is present in the data. The team's conversation is informal but essential to what happens next: asking Exploratory Questions.

Do Second: Ask Exploratory Questions

Exploratory Questions are questions whose answers the teacher team believes will reveal useful information and point it in the direction of identifying learning gaps. They are questions that require additional information to answer and that the team would like to investigate further. They are born from the Wonder Statements in the Notice and Wonder Protocol. In a large way, the Wonder Statements exist for the sole purpose of generating a meaningful Exploratory Question that will drive the remainder of the work in the Data Action Model. Needless to say, the team's choice of an Exploratory Question is critical to yielding strong results for students. If the team generates several significant Exploratory Questions at the same time, it can address them in turn, looping back to address each one individually in a new cycle.

Keep in mind that just because Exploratory Questions come from the Wonder Statements doesn't imply that they are reworded variations of the Wonder Statements. Sometimes this does happen, but more often than not, either the Exploratory Question is a composite of several Wonder Statements, or it was inspired by and derived from one or more of the Wonder Statements. Most important, the Exploratory Question should be significant: *Will answering this question provide the kind of information that will lead to identifying gaps in learning?*

Typically, Exploratory Questions reflect the past, as the following examples show:

- Are we assessing our students' mastery of making inferences from text in a manner consistent with the depth of mastery expected by the PARCC assessments?
- How are we presently teaching quadratic inequalities, and why do our students do so poorly on them?
- Are we spending too much time on drill, and how can we move from teaching primarily procedures to also teaching the concepts behind them, in a manner consistent with the Common Core State Standards for Mathematical Practice?

- How are we presently differentiating instruction on topic *X*, and how might we do it better?
- What, precisely, are the students having difficulty on regarding standard *Y*?

Most of these examples contain the kernel of an implied problem and a curiosity about how to do better or how to fix the problem—which is to be expected. The particular aspects of "the problem" are yet to be determined in any useful way and will be identified in further steps of the Data Action Model, but the "macroproblem" is making itself known through the team's queries. It's not enough to know that the students are performing poorly on test items related to Literal and Interpretive levels (see Figure 4). If we are to "fix the problem," we need to know more specifically which areas in that domain are most problematic and examine with greater scrutiny our current instruction with regard to this strand.

Exploratory Questions require more information to answer. They point to where we will start looking for additional information. They provide a screen for our search, filtering out irrelevant information as we sift through masses of related and unrelated data and extract only those data that address, at least in part, our Exploratory Question. This pursuit of additional data happens between Data Meetings 1 and 2 of the Data Action Model.

Do Third: Decide Who Will Bring What

Now that the teacher team has chosen an Exploratory Question, it's time to gather more information to help the team members answer that question. At the end of Data Meeting 1, the teacher team brainstorms a list of all possible sources of additional data and artifacts that, when analyzed together, will help the team members answer their Exploratory Question.

Calling All Relevant Data

Data sources tapped to answer the team's Exploratory Question are not limited to numerical data in the way of tables and charts, but must include artifacts of teacher and student work. Consider the types of additional data and artifacts listed here:

Additional Data Reports

- Item analysis of a test
- Teacher summary report
- School summary report
- Department summary report
- Student summary report by teacher
- Student summary report by subgroup (gender, race, grade level, English language learners, economically disadvantaged, special needs)
- District versus school summary report

Teacher Work Artifacts

- Curriculum maps
- State/CCSS standards
- Lesson plans
- Unit plans
- Tests and quizzes
- Warm-ups
- Teacher calendar/time line
- Rubrics
- Portfolio requirements
- Writing assignments
- Labs
- Activities and games
- Homework assignments
- Reading assignments
- Teacher grade books

Student Work Artifacts

- Writing samples
- Corrected tests and quizzes
- Student portfolios

- Lab reports
- Student self-evaluations
- Homework
- Classwork
- Electronic work (Prezis, PowerPoints, videos, etc.)
- Student projects
- Student journals/daybooks
- Ticket-out-the-door responses
- Warm-up responses

By viewing these lists through the lens of the Exploratory Question, the teacher team decides which artifacts should be gathered, and by whom, by the time of Data Meeting 2. Of course, not everything listed here will be brought to the next meeting. The team gathers only those items that it deems relevant to answering the Exploratory Question.

The facilitator of the team leads a discussion about who will bring which items to the next team meeting, soliciting volunteers (versus making assignments) to bring the items. Having individual team members commit to bringing their artifacts compels all team members to take ownership in the process and demonstrate commitment to the task of digging deeper into the data toward the eventual goal of improved instruction. This heightened ownership in the process is not a trivial advantage of the team sharing and gathering relevant artifacts. A common concern expressed to me by PLC coaches is that they seem to always be doing all the work themselves. *Each teacher on the team should share the responsibility for any task not directly related to facilitating the team.*

The team follows up this "homework" by reviewing these items—or triangulating additional data. This topic is the work of Data Meeting 2.

From the Trenches

School: Beckham Elementary School
Location: Burney, New Hampshire
Grades: K–5
Demographics: Medium-sized, suburban, middle-SES
Students: 64 percent white, 26 percent students of color, 11 percent eligible for free or reduced lunch
PLC: Grade 3, all subjects, eight teachers plus one assistant principal

Dawn is the coach of the 3rd grade teacher team, and this is the first year she and her team are attempting to use the Data Action Model. They started by looking at PARCC assessment data from the previous year's students and conducted a Notice and Wonder Protocol with it. Many of the team's Wonder Statements focused on the students' performance on items related to asking and answering questions to demonstrate understanding of a text (CCSS.ELA–Literacy.RL.3.1).

The students overall did reasonably well answering the questions, but the teachers wondered just how text-driven their answers really were. Did students know answers because of prior experiences such as classroom discussions on similar text, or were they depending on the text as an informational resource? From their Wonder Statements, the teachers formed a preliminary Exploratory Question: *How proficient are our students at using the text to answer questions about the text?* The question seemed like a reasonable one, but it didn't really lend itself to getting at a constructive result. Simply knowing how proficient students are in their skill is a relatively straightforward bit of information and provides no window of opportunity for student improvement.

Dawn encouraged the PLC members to refine their question to include a connection to their instruction. After a brief but well-focused discussion, the teachers decided on a revised two-part Exploratory Question: *How are we presently instructing students to refer to the text in asking and answering questions, and where can we be more effective in helping them improve their proficiency?*

To answer its question, the team needed more information. Team members needed to fully explore what they were presently doing instructionally to teach this reading skill, and they had to decide at what points during the instruction they could be more effective.

In the last 8 to 10 minutes of Data Meeting 1, the team generated a list of what it needed to have for Data Meeting 2, and Dawn solicited volunteers to bring that material. Items on the teachers' artifacts list included

(continued)

From the Trenches *(continued)*

- Detailed lesson plans from an eight-day unit centered on using text to answer questions;
- Their first-semester curriculum and pacing guides;
- Copies of the district quarterly assessment covering the topic (among others);
- Student work from an assignment on asking questions of an author based on a fictional story;
- Released test items from previous years' PARCC assessment; and
- Short video clips from student performances from an Ask the Experts project on hurricanes and tornadoes.

With all these artifacts available for Data Meeting 2, Dawn and her team felt well positioned to tackle their Exploratory Question.

Data Meeting 2

Triangulating the Data

NOTICE

WONDER

ASK

BRING

TRACK

IDENTIFY

SET

SEARCH

DEVELOP

IMPLEMENT

EVALUATE

Purpose of Triangulation

Triangulating data simply means reviewing additional data with the intent of making clearer connections among three items: (1) our original source of data and the information we extracted from it, (2) our instructional strategies, and (3) our students' performances. In the Data Action Model, triangulation is the process of reviewing additional sources of data to accomplish one of two goals: (1) to corroborate or refute findings that were revealed from previous data sources and noted during the Notice and Wonder Protocol, or (2) to dig into additional data sources to gain greater insights about information we gleaned from previous data sources. The team's primary intention is more often the latter than the former. Because teams have not drawn hard-and-fast conclusions from the data at this point, they triangulate not so much to confirm or refute earlier conclusions as to gain additional information about suspicions that surfaced during the first two steps in the process. Imagine working on a jigsaw puzzle: triangulation is the step in the process where you gather additional pieces of the puzzle mainly to construct a more complete picture, not to confirm your earlier placement of puzzle pieces. The latter may happen during the process, but it is not the impetus behind triangulation.

Do First: Triangulate Additional Data

Of all the steps in the Data Action Model, triangulation is the messiest. There is really no way around it. This is the time when team members bring to the table, literally, a vast array of student and teacher artifacts and other data sources to help them answer their Exploratory Question. There is a method to the madness, however. In the following section, we will discuss one way to work through this morass of teacher and student work.

Tracking Artifacts

At the time of Data Meeting 2, teachers have brought various artifacts—data reports, grade books, and samples of student and teacher work—related to the Exploratory Question. Because this material is dependent on the selected question, there is no cookie-cutter approach as to how teams go about reviewing the material (i.e., triangulating the data). In general, though, teachers should have ample time to sit quietly and independently and review pieces of information, pass them on, or replace them in the center of the table as they take notes about what they see—all the while keeping careful focus on their Exploratory Question. Unlike other data meetings, during which teams complete multiple steps of the Data Action Model, Data Meeting 2 is devoted entirely to triangulating the data by carefully and thoroughly reviewing these artifacts. The 45 minutes that a teacher team may spend doing this will potentially save hours of unnecessary, unfocused, or ineffective work later on.

In training PLC coaches and team leaders to use the Data Action Model with their teams, one of the questions I am most commonly asked is "Can you offer us a systematic way for reviewing this stuff?" Unfortunately, as mentioned, because "this stuff" varies so much, a one-size-fits-all process is not possible. However, I *can* offer the template shown in Figure 5, which helps make this messy job a bit neater (a larger version of this figure is available for your use in the Appendix, p. 142).

Because triangulation leads to the work to be done during Data Meeting 3 on identifying learning and instructional gaps, I have found it useful to make these gaps a focus of the Artifact Tracking Sheet. During this step in which teachers bring and review additional information, they are not simply looking at it; they are looking for clues to help identify gaps. This is where the work of Data Meetings 2 and 3 blends seamlessly together. While team

— Figure 5 —

Artifact Tracking Sheet			
Artifact Type (be specific) • Data table • Student work • Teacher lesson plan(s) • Teacher instruction calendar • Test items • Unit plan	**Observed Learning Gap** (as evidenced by artifact) ***or*** **Observed Instructional Gap** (as evidenced by artifact)	**Relative Significance** (if learning gap observed) *How important is this skill/concept?*	**Prominence** (if learning gap observed) *Speculate as to how widespread this gap is with all the students.*
	LG IG	1 2 3 4 5	1 2 3 4 5
	LG IG	1 2 3 4 5	1 2 3 4 5
	LG IG	1 2 3 4 5	1 2 3 4 5
	LG IG	1 2 3 4 5	1 2 3 4 5
	LG IG	1 2 3 4 5	1 2 3 4 5
	LG IG	1 2 3 4 5	1 2 3 4 5
	LG IG	1 2 3 4 5	1 2 3 4 5
	LG IG	1 2 3 4 5	1 2 3 4 5
	LG IG	1 2 3 4 5	1 2 3 4 5
	LG IG	1 2 3 4 5	1 2 3 4 5

members are looking at the additional data, they are keeping track of learning and instructional gaps as they present themselves in the process. The team will then pinpoint specific, targeted learning gaps during Data Meeting 3 and connect those gaps to the correlated instructional gaps. For now, the team members list all they can and care to as they triangulate the additional pieces of information through the lens of their Exploratory Question.

To get a sense of what kinds of items and notes might be listed on the Artifact Tracking Sheet, consider the examples compiled on the form in Figure 6. Typically, the items that the team lists on the tracking sheet reflect a mix of observations relevant to the Exploratory Question, some of these being learner weaknesses and others being instructional weaknesses. Most often, each teacher on the team fills out several Artifact Tracking Sheets during the triangulation step. Also, it is not uncommon for one tracking sheet to contain several observations that all pertain to a single artifact.

— **Figure 6** —

Sample Completed Artifact Tracking Sheet

Artifact Type (be specific) • Data table • Student work • Teacher lesson plan(s) • Teacher instruction calendar • Test items • Unit plan	**Observed Learning Gap** (as evidenced by artifact) ***or*** **Observed Instructional Gap** (as evidenced by artifact)	**Relative Significance** (if learning gap observed) *How important is this skill/concept?*	**Prominence** (if learning gap observed) *Speculate as to how widespread this gap is with all the students.*
Data report by substrand	**LG** IG drawing inferences from text	1 2 3 4 **5**	1 2 3 **4** 5
Lesson plan on mitosis	LG **IG** too few illustrations	1 2 3 4 5	1 2 3 4 5
Essay on power	**LG** IG weak transitions	1 2 3 **4** 5	1 2 3 **4** 5
Teacher calendar	LG **IG** too few days on ∆s	1 2 3 4 5	1 2 3 4 5
Student vocab quiz	**LG** IG incorrect usage	1 2 **3** 4 5	1 2 **3** 4 5
Teacher test on quadratics	LG **IG** too many MC, too few CR	1 2 3 4 5	1 2 3 4 5
Student notebook on Ch. 4	**LG** IG too much copying; no understanding	1 2 3 4 **5**	1 2 3 **4** 5
" " " "	LG **IG** are we writing too little?	1 2 3 4 5	1 2 3 4 5
Student test on Civil War	**LG** IG weak essay	1 2 3 **4** 5	1 2 3 4 **5**
" " " "	**LG** IG poor argumentation	1 2 3 4 **5**	1 2 3 **4** 5

It is worth pointing out that not all learning gaps can possibly be noted on the Artifact Tracking Sheets. A single artifact, such as a student test, often has a host of errors, gaps, and misunderstandings, depending on the student whose paper it is. Here again, when teacher teams focus their observations on their Exploratory Question, they filter out irrelevant gaps—significant though they may be—and produce a streamlined composite of gaps related to the question they themselves sought to answer. Otherwise, the result can be a long shopping list of often-unrelated gaps that provides no real usefulness in targeting specific instructional areas for improvement. I tell PLCs, "If everything's important, then nothing's important."

In cases where lots of relevant learning gaps are evident, teachers should record on the tracking sheet the problems they deem most important or that are most likely to crop up among other students. Because teachers will note all learning gaps related to the Exploratory Question, it stands to reason that some gaps will be more important than others. The last two columns of the Artifact Tracking Sheet provide space for teachers to rate the significance (i.e., how important) and prominence (i.e., how widespread) of the gaps they have noted. These ratings are subjective; there is no rubric delineating exactly what a rating of "1" represents, for example. This prioritizing of which gaps to note and which to ignore works to the good of the team because the final collection of noted gaps winds up being those of most significance to the team. This effect encourages solidarity within the team, particularly when it comes time to set goals for students and create an action plan for teachers.

Each meeting of the Data Action Model leads to the next. The first half of the model (Data Meetings 1–3) involves reviewing the data: digging into the data to really explore what is happening with student learning and identify gaps. The second half (Data Meetings 4 and 5) involves responding to what has been learned in the first half: setting goals, making a plan and deciding on an evaluation measure, implementing the plan, and assessing the plan's effectiveness. Arguably, the first half of the model requires more PLC meeting time than the second half. Most of the tasks in the second half happen outside the meeting room and in the classroom. For this reason, by the time teams finish triangulating the data in Data Meeting 2, they may feel as though they still have a long way to go. In actuality, they have spent at least half of the time required to complete all necessary steps of the model. In addition, the collection of completed Artifact Tracking Sheets teams have at the end of Data Meeting 2 moves them seamlessly into the work of the next meeting: identifying learning and instructional gaps. This is the subject of Data Meeting 3: Determining Gaps and Goals.

From the Trenches

School: Robert L. Evans Middle School (REMS)
Location: Polk, Iowa
Grades: 6–8
Demographics: Small, rural, middle-SES
Students: 92 percent white, 8 percent students of color, 24 percent eligible for free or reduced lunch
PLC: Grade 7, social studies, four teachers plus the principal

The 7th grade social studies team at REMS includes four social studies teachers and the principal of REMS, Dr. Leslie Miller, who is a former middle school social studies teacher. The team is coached by Joyce, who has done so since receiving her coach's training two years ago. Dr. Miller was trained along with Joyce and knows that her role on the team is more as a colleague than as school principal.

Since the CCSS came out, the team has wrestled with student mastery of ELA Literacy Standard RH.6–8.2, getting students to identify key ideas from text that are separate from students' opinions or prior knowledge. As a team, they arrived at the following Exploratory Question during Data Meeting 1: *In what specific ways are we currently instructing students to identify key ideas from text that are separate from their opinions, and where do their root difficulties lie in attempting to do so?*

In preparation for Data Meeting 2, the Social Studies 7 PLC rounded up artifacts for triangulation, including

- Student essays from three separate assignments;
- A unit test on main ideas;
- Two short quiz results specifically addressing the role of opinion in judgment;
- Samples of student homework and in-class assignments; and
- All relevant texts that students had been using as primary and secondary sources.

In addition, team members brought lesson plans from the unit, including PowerPoint and Prezi presentations, a video clip of Congress from C-SPAN, and the requirements of an in-class project on debates.

Joyce led her PLC through the triangulation process, reminding teachers that they were to note on their Artifact Tracking Sheets only those gaps relevant to their Exploratory Question. She kept discussion to a minimum, responding to comments with "Make a note of it." All members were engaged in the process, and artifacts were continually reviewed and replaced in the center of the table while the team worked. Joyce concluded the process after 40 minutes and quickly went over what would happen at the next meeting so that all the teachers would be prepared.

Data Meeting 3

Determining Gaps and Goals

NOTICE

WONDER

ASK

BRING

TRACK

IDENTIFY

SET

SEARCH

DEVELOP

IMPLEMENT

EVALUATE

In Data Meeting 2, the teacher team spent a good deal of time sifting through student and teacher artifacts that helped paint a clearer picture of what is happening with student learning. The team members' Exploratory Question has driven this process: all revelations that were uncovered specifically addressed the Exploratory Question. Think of triangulation as the step in which new clues are gathered to help explain more thoroughly what is happening around the issues raised by the Exploratory Question. If PLCs spend adequate time sifting through these artifacts, processing what they're seeing, and noting learning and instructional gaps, then the next tasks of the Data Action Model should follow seamlessly.

Do First: Identify Learning Gaps

Student learning gaps get recorded on the Artifact Tracking Sheet during the triangulation step (see Figure 6, p. 42). Some gaps recorded will be relatively insignificant. For example, in pursuing artifacts related to an Exploratory Question about why students struggle in writing evidence-based persuasive essays, a learning gap on appropriate citation of Internet sources may be relatively insignificant in the bigger scheme of things. It's not that knowing how to cite Internet sources is *not* important, but taking action to correct this gap does little to address the Exploratory Question on writing evidence-based persuasive essays; therefore, this gap is a distraction to the team's main focus.

Other gaps recorded on the Artifact Tracking Sheet will be representative of only a handful of students and not prominent throughout the class.

Continuing with the previous ELA example, in reviewing a particular sample of student work, teachers may notice students' misuse of argument by appeal to authority. Although the gap pertains to the team's Exploratory Question and should be noted on the Artifact Tracking Sheet, it may be an issue with only a small group of students. That is, the gap, although *significant,* may not be *prominent.* Again, as mentioned in Data Meeting 2, it is useful to record a numerical rating of each gap's significance and prominence. Although both of these ratings are subjective, they help the teacher teams focus on the most important and widespread gaps they are observing. This is not to say that the other gaps are unimportant; it is the team members who must decide whether and to what extent they will address these gaps.

Many learning gaps uncovered and recorded from sifting through the artifacts will be both significant and prominent. These are the gaps that significantly affect the answer to the Exploratory Question and that are widespread throughout the population of students. Moreover, these gaps are likely to be noted independently by several members of the PLC as they examine artifacts. In fact, one of the defining characteristics of a prominent gap is that it is noted by more than one teacher; this is a testament to its prominence. All of these indicators make for a relatively easy decision to target these learning gaps for further exploration and action for improvement.

Do Second: Identify Instructional Gaps

Identifying instructional gaps may *seem* like the logical next step, but it has been my experience in working with teacher teams that they all too often skip this essential step. PLCs are often comfortable identifying gaps in their students' learning and then moving swiftly to a plan of action for their students. The problem with this approach lies in teachers' failure to connect the observed student gaps with what it is they themselves are (or are not) doing in the classroom. Without connecting observed gaps in students' learning to teachers' behaviors, we become hard-pressed as educators to create plausible plans of action that will remediate those learning gaps. We must look at our instruction if we are to make changes that affect student learning. Otherwise, the conversation becomes centered on what the students aren't doing, on what the students can't do, on what the students don't know, on what the students didn't learn last year, and so forth. All of these factors are related and important, but their existence most often follows corollarily from what it is that *we* are or are not doing. In my experience, the teacher teams that make the greatest strides in instructional improvement are those that are comfortable looking regularly at their practice and with sufficient scrutiny so as to make meaningful changes.

Linking Learning Gaps to Instructional Gaps

There often comes a point during data discussions about learning gaps in which team members spend an inordinate amount of time talking about things over which they have little or no control. Undoubtedly, comments such as "Ten of the 27 students in my class have IEPs," "More than half of the 8th grade students in Applied Science are reading at a 4th grade level," or "My English language learners are illiterate in their own native language" reflect genuine impediments to student learning. Sadly, they are also matters over which teachers have little control. Teachers often wind up making statements like these not because they are reluctant to accept responsibility for their students' learning; my experience points to the contrary. Rather, making such observations seems to be a natural tendency when overworked, underpaid, and well-intentioned teachers come together and discuss possible reasons why their students are underperforming in certain areas. Understandable though this behavior may be, it can also lead teacher teams down a path of helplessness and squandered time, and the result is a general lack of productivity.

When this common but potentially derailing phenomenon occurs, PLC facilitators are often at their wit's end to bring the conversation back to a more productive exchange. The challenge in doing this often lies in the fact that the problems teachers identify, while out of their control, are real obstacles that *do* inhibit classroom instruction and student learning. To dismiss such concerns or treat them as invalid would be unfair to teachers. So, to help reel in teachers when the conversation turns to external forces, I refer to the graphic in Figure 7, which I often sketch on chart paper or a whiteboard during data meetings. I use it to call the team's attention to the fact that some of the obstacles being discussed, while valid and significant, hover in the outer region of "no direct or indirect influence." We stand to make the biggest difference for our students when we focus on the obstacles in those areas where we have at least some influence. Of course, the graphic is not a panacea to address wayward discussions, and it clearly does not address the real external forces that teachers may have mentioned, but it does remind teachers that some obstacles *are* subject to our direct or indirect influence. When more pessimistic teachers claim that they have influence over very few obstacles, I generally retort that it should be easy in that case to list them—and so we do.

— Figure 7 —

Circles of Influence

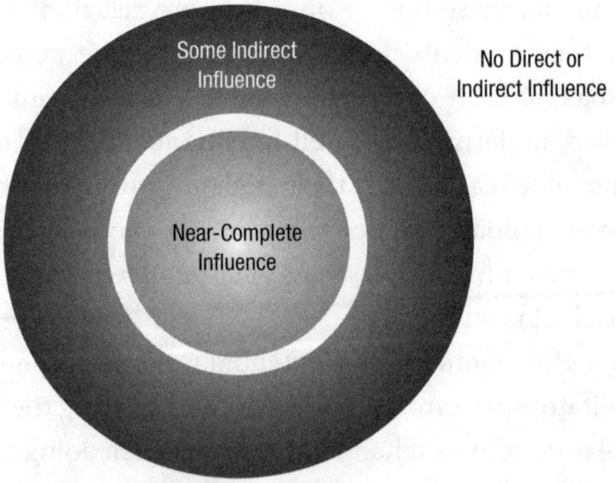

Listing the Gaps

After teacher team members have discussed the student learning gaps of greatest prominence and significance, using their Artifact Tracking Sheets as a guide, they list these in the left column of a two-column Google document or on a whiteboard or chart paper. In the right column, they list any instructional gaps they cited that are connected to the recorded student learning gaps. For example, a team may list "trouble solving equations when the variable is on the right side of the equation" under "Student Learning Gaps," and then write "insufficient practice with equations whose variable is on the right side" under the "Instructional Gaps" column. This example may seem simplistic, especially since it has an obvious solution: providing more practice to the students. However, it is not uncommon for both learning gaps and instructional gaps to be remedied just that simply, and therefore they should be noted in the document so that their fix does indeed wind up in the Data Action Plan (see Data Meeting 4).

Once the PLC has spent 30 minutes or so discussing instructional gaps and aligning them to the identified learning gaps, it's time for the team to articulate a goal.

Do Third: Set a Target Learning Goal

As is the case with many steps in the Data Action Model, if the team does a good job with any one step, the next step generally follows with little effort. Setting a Target Learning Goal is an obvious extension of identifying student learning gaps. At this point in the model, the teachers in the PLC are not concerning themselves with how the goal may best be achieved but only with setting the goal. The goal set by the teacher team may or may not be a *SMART goal*. The SMART acronym refers to a goal that is *s*pecific, *m*easurable, *a*ttainable, *r*elevant, and *t*ime-bound (Doran, Miller, & Cunningham, 1981). Consider each of these SMART attributes in the context of the Data Action Model as presented in Figure 8.

— Figure 8 —

SMART Goals in Context	
SMART Characteristic	**Application to Data Action Model**
Specific	The goal is appropriately sized. Avoid goals that are too granular or too general.
Measurable	The goal is measurable, at least subjectively. If a goal is not measurable, there is no clear way to determine whether it has been reached.
Attainable	The goal is reachable. For example, stating that 100 percent of students will read on grade level by a certain date may sound appealing but may not be realistic, depending on factors like students' current reading level, the number of English language learners, and so forth.
Relevant	The goal directly addresses identified learning gaps.
Time-bound	There is a target completion date for the goal. (Details of the time line will be addressed in the Data Action Plan during Data Meeting 4.)

Here are some examples of SMART Target Learning Goals:

- The percentage of 7th grade students meeting or exceeding the standard in operations with fractions will increase by 30 percent.
- At least 80 percent of 4th grade students will score a 3 or 4 on the Writing Rubric dimension "Citing Evidence from Text."
- At least 60 percent of Algebra 2 students will be able to solve problems involving exponential functions in nonroutine contexts with at least 75 percent accuracy in final answers and 90 percent accuracy in their approach.
- By the end of the first quarter, 100 percent of 1st grade students will be able to use their student dictionaries to look up new and unfamiliar words.

Do Fourth: Decide on an Evaluation Metric

The final task for the teacher team to complete during Data Meeting 3 is to decide how it will know whether it has achieved its goal. This next step may seem obvious, but I have witnessed many instances of teams setting a goal and then immediately pursuing the goal with no clear sense of how they will know whether and when they have reached their goal. In these cases, teams proceed with a vague sense of the stopping point of the data cycle and with an equally vague aim at their Target Learning Goal. Therefore, it is important for teams to decide on an evaluation metric for their goal before they begin pursuing it. This recommendation is akin to teachers writing assessments on an upcoming unit before instruction begins. Writing assessments ahead of instruction keeps instruction focused on the goal.

In nearly all cases, the evaluation metric most commonly used is some type of student assessment. After all, if we are trying to decide whether the goal set for students has been reached, some form of assessment of our students' learning is the most logical way to do so. This assessment may be a teacher-designed test, a textbook post-test, a portion of a standardized test, or a quiz covering the content described in the learning goal. It may be relatively short, like a 10-question quiz, or it may be a culminating project or presentation or virtually any performance-based assessment. It may be written, oral, or digital in format. It may be given to the class as a whole or administered to students individually or in small groups. The point is that the assessment should measure whether or not the Target Learning Goal has been achieved. Precisely how this evaluation is done is less important than the fact that it is done.

As teachers who have worked with me know, I am a big advocate of "less is more" in most educational realms, especially when it comes to assessments. If a 10-question quiz can adequately assess student mastery and provide reliable evidence that a goal was or was not reached, I'm all for that. Teachers are too busy to burden themselves with writing long and elaborate assessments to measure their learning goals. If the job can be done simply, briefly, and reliably, then that is how they ought to do it. Teachers who use a pre-test before they begin instruction (often provided by the publisher of whatever materials they are using) can modify the pre-test to use later as an evaluation metric.

Once the team has set the goal and chosen the mechanism to assess how well the goal was reached, it is time to design an action plan that will be carried out where it matters most: in the classroom. This is the subject of the next chapter.

From the Trenches

School: Bloing-Hart Elementary School (BHES)
Location: Jacksonville, Florida
Grades: K–5
Demographics: Large, urban, low-SES, Title I
Students: 11 percent white, 89 percent students of color, more than 75 percent eligible for free or reduced lunch
PLC: Grade 5, all subjects, 10 teachers plus 1 reading specialist

Ms. Williams coaches the 5th grade learning team (as PLCs are called at BHES), which consists of 10 5th grade teachers and a reading specialist, Dana Deckert. Learning teams were established four years ago by the then-new principal, Claudia Garcia, and each is led by a trained coach. Along with help from Ms. Deckert, Ms. Williams has been coaching the grade 5 learning team for two years. This year, per Dr. Garcia's mandate, all learning teams are focused on using data to inform their instruction and on applying the steps outlined in the Data Action Model.

Ms. Williams faced several challenges with her team. First, the grade 5 team is a large group that includes several teachers who have been at BHES for at least 10 years. Two teachers on her team have been with the school for almost 20 years. Because Ms. Williams has only been teaching for seven years herself, the dynamics of the group can at times be difficult for her to address. Another challenge is the fact that many of the team's teachers are intimidated by data, and several are quick to claim that they've gotten by fine for years without "doing so much data stuff."

The Data Action Model has helped the teachers become less "dataphobic" as they proceed systematically through the defined steps governing what they should be doing. Ms. Williams has guided them nicely through each step, and most of the team has been on board with the meetings. Particularly sensitive to the veteran teachers, Ms. Williams solicits their input and opinions at every opportunity.

During Data Meeting 3, the learning team zoomed in on learning gaps in science that addressed their Exploratory Question from the previous meeting. The team members decided that their students were struggling with proposing solutions to scientific issues. The students showed reasonable proficiency in assessing various solutions based on scientific findings but had great difficulty in proposing their own scientifically based solutions.

However, when it came time to list instructional gaps that aligned to these student weaknesses, the learning team fell short. Most of the teacher gaps shared had to do with things like spending too little time on proposing solutions or not giving students enough practice proposing solutions based on scientific evidence. These instructional gaps were noteworthy, but not sufficiently reflective to formulate a significant goal or to fix the problem.

From the Trenches *(continued)*

Ms. Williams pushed her learning team to reflect on *how* they were teaching proposing solutions and less on how much time they spent on this activity. She asked them questions like these: *If students had to write a rubric for scoring good scientific solutions to problems, could they do it? How would we teach them about proposing solutions so that they could do this, without giving them a list of criteria?*

From that discussion, which was centered on *how* the teachers were teaching the skill, the learning team formulated a goal that articulated student understanding of proposing solutions and decided that they would use Ms. Williams's idea for an evaluation metric. They would ask students to create their own rubric for developing solutions to scientifically based problems, ranging from the BP oil spill in the Gulf of Mexico, to the overpopulation of eelpout in Alaskan lakes, to the near-extinction of tigers in East Africa. If the students could do this task well, the team decided, the teachers would know whether they had reached their goal. Exactly how they would meet this goal would be the subject of Data Meeting 4.

Data Meeting 4

Planning for Action

NOTICE

WONDER

ASK

BRING

TRACK

IDENTIFY

SET

SEARCH

DEVELOP

IMPLEMENT

EVALUATE

In Data Meeting 2, the teacher team examined a conglomerate of data artifacts related to its Exploratory Question. In Data Meeting 3, the team pinpointed specific learning gaps as well as the corresponding instructional gaps and then crafted a Target Learning Goal that set out to "correct" the identified learning gap(s). In this most recent meeting, the team focused mostly on what the students were not mastering or not mastering sufficiently; the teachers' own actions came up only in the context of the instructional gaps that corresponded to the learning gaps. In this way, Data Meeting 3 resulted in the team deciding the "end game"—that is, what level of success they would like to see their students achieve and by when.

In contrast, Data Meeting 4 focuses almost exclusively on what the teachers themselves need to do to reach the goal they established in the previous meeting. That is, during this data meeting, the teacher team will establish the *means* necessary to achieve the desired goal. To do this well, the PLC must do a bit of homework.

Do Prior: Conduct a Strategies Search

Albert Einstein is often credited with the observation that insanity is "'doing the same thing over and over again and expecting different results." Teachers and administrators have no monopoly on this behavior, but it does happen in education with unfortunate regularity. The point of Data Meeting 4 is to develop an instructional plan of action that will help significantly assuage, if not eradicate, students' targeted learning gaps. This presupposes our intention to do something *different* in the classroom—and not to do the same thing over and over again. The hitch in this reasonable-sounding intention is this: as teachers, we have already taught the particular standard in question as best we know how. If that initial approach didn't work, and students still have learning gaps, do we then teach our *second-best* lesson on the topic? Surely not. We need something new.

With a little legwork, this conundrum is easily solved. In order to improve their instruction and be more successful with students regarding the standard in question, the members of the teacher team need to find new strategies, new lessons, and new activities. I call this gathering of new materials a *Strategies Search*. This process pushes teachers to be innovative and find new ways of teaching familiar topics. The only way we can improve our instruction and, by extension, our students' learning, is to try something new—at least new for us.

Between the end of Data Meeting 3 and the start of Data Meeting 4, each member of the PLC should do some homework, searching digital and print resources to find one or two new strategies or activities to enhance instruction in the standard where the team observed the learning gap. Given the plethora of resources available for teachers today, particularly on the Internet, it is generally fairly easy to find *something* that will apply to the targeted learning gap. To be sure, not every activity found is going to be good. Any teacher can post anything on the Internet, and not every idea will translate into an activity that is effective, appropriate, or structurally suited to every group of students. For every strong, impactful lesson or activity found on any given topic on the Internet, there are probably four or five that are not appropriate or of high quality. Still, good stuff is out there. Locating it simply requires teacher teams to take the time to find it.

It is important for the team coach or facilitator to insist that all members bring something new to the table for Data Meeting 4. Otherwise, teams find themselves spinning their wheels looking at the same old activities—many of which proved to be unhelpful the first time. In cases when the identified learning gap affects or encompasses several standards, teams can divide the homework of searching for strategies by standard so that all players are working to cover all bases.

Do First: Review Strategies and Activities

At the start of Data Meeting 4, team members begin to take a critical look at the host of new strategies and activities they discovered. Not all strategies or lesson activities are created equal. Some activities result in a great impact on student learning, whereas others have little or no effect on learning or achievement. Every seasoned teacher has tried activities that were engaging for students, heightening their motivation and interest, but that left much to be desired in terms of what students actually *learned*. I'm reminded of what I have come to call "Flashy Poster Syndrome": students work for days, in and out of class, producing colorful posters on the topic being taught. Sometimes the posters are spectacular, and the learning inherent in producing them is clear. In many other instances, however, the posters, while eye-catching, reveal very little student learning. I first became aware of Flashy Poster Syndrome in my 9th grade math class, when I would ask my students to prepare posters related to some topic we were studying. When students presented their posters to the class, I noticed that the posters contained fancy lettering, lots of colors, and an abundance of graphics. Sometimes they were even chock-full of content. Yet the students had trouble answering even the simplest questions about the content. The project that I had thought was so engaging ended up being more about copying and nicely packaging bits of information than about building and demonstrating conceptual knowledge of the topic.

To avoid Flashy Poster Syndrome (and its equivalent in other content delivery methods), teacher teams need a metric for deciding which activities or lesson components stand to have the greatest impact on student learning. To this end, I have developed the Planning Protocol.

The Planning Protocol

The primary litmus test deciding whether a learning activity is meaningful is being able to provide a solid answer to the question *What are students learning from this?* If the activity is designed to formatively assess students, the question becomes *What are students demonstrating they have learned by doing this?* The actual learning target is not for students to make a poster or a PowerPoint presentation; the goal is for students either to gain new understanding or to show evidence of newly gained understanding.

The Planning Protocol is a tool that helps the teacher team sort through possible lesson components (strategies, activities, and tasks) and keep only those of the highest quality, as determined by the rubric in Figure 9. (You can find an overview of the entire protocol on pages 116–118 in the Appendix). In addition to reviewing (Step 1) and scoring (Step 2) the lesson components, the PLC members also have an opportunity in Step 3 of the Planning Protocol to make suggestions for improving any lesson components that they may have given a low score but that have the *potential* to make a significant impact on student learning. In this way, the team doesn't just review lesson components; it actually *improves* those components in the dimensions where they are lacking. The net result is higher-quality lessons.

— Figure 9 —

Planning Protocol Rubric

Dimension	1	2	3	4
Alignment to Standards	Barely or not at all aligned	Somewhat aligned	Mostly aligned	Completely aligned
Impact on Learning	Low impact	Medium-low impact	Medium-high impact	High impact
Student Engagement	Low student engagement likely	Moderate engagement for some students	Moderate engagement for most students	High engagement for most students
Depth of Knowledge	Recall	Skill/concept	Strategic reasoning	Extended reasoning
Technology Integration	Opportunities to integrate technology overlooked	Use of some technology	Effective and prominent use of technology	Effective and innovative use of technology
Teacher Friendliness		High maintenance (lots of materials and prep work)	Low maintenance (few materials and/or little prep work)	
Rigor and Relevance	Teacher works	Students work	Students think	Students think and work

The Planning Protocol offers another important benefit. When team members work together to discuss and evaluate work—whether teacher work or student work—they develop a common knowledge base and common expectation for what they mean by quality work (in this case, activities or lesson components). This common understanding that results from the team working together in real time (as opposed to working on the same task separately and then coming together after the fact) is what I refer to as "constructing community knowledge" (Venables, 2011). Constructing community knowledge is an effective and powerful way to build both buy-in and solidarity among PLC members. When all constituents review, score, and discuss the same piece of work together, their individual and collective understanding of attributes such as *rigor, impact on learning, student engagement,* and *alignment to standards* converges to the same. This impact makes the team stronger and the work it produces better.

Do Second: Develop a Data Action Plan

After the PLC has reviewed lesson components and decided which ones are of highest quality based on the rubric in the Planning Protocol, it's time to create an action plan. Whereas a Target Learning Goal focuses the team on the behavior and performance of students, the Data Action Plan focuses the team on the behavior and performances of teachers, particularly during instruction. The Target Learning Goal is the end; the actionable items in the Data Action Plan are the means.

To help tie these actionable items together in a cohesive plan of action, and in a manner that preserves the SMART attributes discussed in the previous chapter, I have developed an Action Plan Tracking Sheet (see Figure 10; a larger version is available for your use in the Appendix, p. 143). In the top line of this tracking sheet, the team states the Target Learning Goal and, in the bottom line, the evaluation metric for assessing the team's success in reaching that goal as well as a completion date. Recall that both the goal and the evaluation metric were decided on in Data Meeting 3.

— Figure 10 —

Action Plan Tracking Sheet					
GOAL:					
Instructional Tactic (be specific) *What will be done?*	**Tactic Method** *Specifically how will it be done?*	**Acting Party** *Who will do it?*	**Frequency** *How often will this task be done?*	**Completion Date**	**Verifying Artifacts** Which artifacts will serve as evidence that the instructional tactic has been implemented?
Evaluation Metric					

The columns in the Action Plan Tracking Sheet are completed as follows:

Instructional tactic. In this column, the team lists the names of the various instructional activities and other lesson components that it has given high scores using the Planning Protocol rubric. These are the components that team members have agreed to implement.

Tactic method. The tactic method specifies how the instructional tactic will be conducted. For example, will students work in groups? If so, how will the groups be arranged? Will students finish tasks outside class if they are short on time in class? What provisions will the teacher make for students of differing abilities? Anything relevant to the execution of the instructional tactic is noted under this heading.

Acting party. In most cases, all of the teachers in the team will be the acting party for each instructional tactic. However, sometimes only a few individuals will conduct certain aspects of the action plan. For example, a member of the team whose expertise is working with students with disabilities may be the only acting party for a particular instructional tactic.

Frequency. Some instructional tactics will recur throughout the Implementation Period (e.g., weekly or at the end of the relevant period each day), while others occur only once. In either case, the team notes the frequency with which the tactics will be used.

Completion date. This date helps the team keep in mind that the work listed in the Data Action Plan—not just the Target Learning Goal—is time-bound. Not all tactics will be implemented the same day, or even the same week, so the team chooses a target completion date for each tactic.

Verifying artifacts. As part of the action plan, the team decides which artifacts will serve as evidence that each instructional tactic has been implemented and that the goal has been met. Artifacts might include student work, teacher lesson plans, completed assessments, videos of student presentations, student posters, and even homework papers. Collecting and keeping track of supporting artifacts and sharing them at meetings add an element of accountability for all teachers on the team. Anything that encourages the tactics in the action plan to be realized in the classroom helps ensure that the plan isn't mere lip service paid by well-intentioned teachers.

Once the team completes the Action Plan Tracking Sheet, it is important that team members follow up by checking in and providing updates at the start of each PLC meeting during the Implementation Period (the subject of the next chapter). This follow-up sends the message to all teachers on the team that the work is important and that *deciding* action must be followed by actually *taking* action.

From the Trenches

School: Caballo Cruce High School (CCHS)
Location: San Diego, California
Grades: 9–12
Demographics: Large, urban, low-SES, Title I
Students: 58 percent white, 42 percent students of color, 45 percent eligible for free or reduced lunch
PLC: Grades 9 and 10, biology, seven teachers plus one special education teacher

The Biology PLC consists of teachers who teach both 9th and 10th grade sections of biology. The curriculum is the same for both sections, although the students are not. The 9th grade students are accelerated, and the teachers on the team consider the 9th graders' sections the "honors sections," although the classes are not formally designated as such. The Biology PLC, like all subject-based PLCs at CCHS, meets after school weekly. Mrs. Vasquez coaches the team. The principal, Cesar Contreras, asked her to take on this responsibility at the end of last year. This is the first year of "formal" PLCs at CCHS.

The year has been bumpy at times, and Mrs. Vasquez has been challenged by the tension of balancing the needs of the group with the needs of individual team members, some of whom have not fully embraced the notion of authentic PLCs. As at many high schools across the United States, teachers at CCHS have in the past enjoyed a degree of autonomy in their planning and in their teaching. Things changed when Mr. Contreras became principal two years ago.

In previous data meetings, the team members identified gaps in students' knowledge and understanding of cellular transcription and translation, a multistep process that contains a good deal of new vocabulary for the students. As a team—with some trepidation—the teachers set a goal that at least 75 percent of the 10th grade biology students and 85 percent of the 9th grade biology students would show 70 percent mastery on the standard in question, as measured by a post-test that the team would create at the onset of the unit.

In preparation for Data Meeting 4, the team had agreed to conduct a Strategies Search, with each teacher bringing back to the group one new lesson idea or activity designed to instruct students on the standard. Two teachers came unprepared to share anything. One team member shared an idea for an activity related to the topic but offered no details for implementation. The other four teachers collectively came up with five activities, including

- An activity in which students create a comic strip that identifies the steps of the cellular transcription and translation process and whose characters narrate the steps' purpose;
- An activity that asks students to write newspaper "help wanted" ads for each topic-related vocabulary word;
- A card-sort activity for each vocabulary word;

From the Trenches *(continued)*

• An activity in which students write predictions for what would fail and why if a randomly selected vocabulary word (e.g., *ribosome*) were eliminated from the process; and

• An activity asking students to write their own assessments on the topic and then to exchange and grade them.

After team members quietly reviewed the activities, Mrs. Vasquez led them in a discussion of each activity idea using the rubric in the Planning Protocol (Figure 9), probing teachers to explore why each activity received the scores it did. Some members disagreed with one another on scores given in certain dimensions of some activities, but the discussion was productive in several ways. First, all members of the PLC felt engaged in the process and were eager to use the rubric to score the activities—even those teachers who had brought nothing to the table. In this way, individual teacher buy-in was high.

Second, Mrs. Vasquez was particularly skillful in reminding team members that they were scoring the *activity,* not the teacher who had brought the activity. Highlighting this important distinction before teachers began scoring helped ensure that no teacher felt discounted if the work he or she had brought happened to earn low scores. One teacher even prefaced her idea with the observation, "I don't think this strategy is great, but I did like this one aspect of it."

Finally, the teachers ended up being harsh scorers, which served to up the ante for the team as a whole in terms of striving for high-quality activities and lesson components. Mrs. Vasquez was pleasantly surprised.

Once the team had decided to try a few of the activities and tweaked another one, the teachers began to write their Data Action Plan, including their chosen activities as the instructional tactics. It was smooth sailing from here; the PLC completed the Action Plan Tracking Sheet in less than 20 minutes. Mrs. Vasquez then led a debriefing of Data Meeting 4 with her team. She left the meeting feeling confident that the teachers were all beginning to get on board and were more united as a team at the end of the meeting than at the onset.

Implementation Period

In the Classroom

NOTICE

WONDER

ASK

BRING

TRACK

IDENTIFY

SET

SEARCH

DEVELOP

IMPLEMENT

EVALUATE

Implementing the Data Action Plan

The process of implementing the Data Action Model to this point has been deliberate, focused, and, at times, necessarily messy. By the conclusion of Data Meeting 4, the PLC has spent many hours as a team and several hours individually carefully reviewing student data, student work, and teacher work. Team members have identified gaps and goals in learning and instruction. They have also designed a well-researched Data Action Plan (complete with evaluation metric).

The PLC has already accomplished a lot. But unless changes happen at the classroom level, all the work the PLC has done to this point will largely be in vain. Data used to inform but not alter our practice are useless data. During the next month (or less), the teachers in the PLC will move from data that have been *informative* to data that are *impactful.*

The Next Four Weeks

As I have pointed out, the Data Action Model generally takes up to nine weeks to cycle through. The first four weeks are spent reviewing the data, isolating gaps, and planning for action; the next four weeks are spent implementing the Data Action Plan; and the final week is used to evaluate the success of the plan based on a predetermined metric and according to the new data generated by implementation.

The whole cycle can also take as few as three or four weeks, depending on how often PLCs meet and for how long, the size of the goal being pursued in the action plan, and the length of the Implementation Period. If the decided classroom changes or strategies can be fully implemented in a week, there is no need to drag out the process. For our purposes, however, and for the sake of clarity, we will assume that the cycle in discussion is the more typical nine-week cycle and that the PLC is meeting once a week for 60 minutes.

During the four weeks of the Implementation Period, each teacher in the PLC carries out the instructional tactics that make up the Data Action Plan. While these strategies are being executed in the classroom, the PLC continues to meet weekly. During these meetings, the teacher team looks at teacher work and student work, engages in text-based discussions, and reviews formative data that emerge during the Implementation Period. These meetings are crucial to the success of the Data Action Plan. They give the PLC the opportunity to monitor progress and gain new knowledge that may be needed in successfully implementing the Data Action Plan.

For example, if a teacher team has decided that it is not doing enough in the way of differentiating lessons, and if team members' foundational knowledge of differentiation is inadequate, discussing a book chapter on the topic would be appropriate and a good use of meeting time (see, e.g., Tomlinson, 2004). In addition to text-based discussions, teacher teams can spend these critical meetings examining teacher and student work so that they are abreast of what is working and what is not. These meetings can serve as an effective check-in point while teachers try strategies from the Data Action Plan in the classroom.

This ongoing process of trying strategies and determining their effectiveness in the short term keeps the team focused on achievement of the Target Learning Goal set during Data Meeting 3. Teacher teams also become invested in a culture of using data to target learning and instructional gaps and changing instruction to deliver more promising student results. When these endeavors happen at the team level, with dialogue and input from all members of the team, individual teacher commitment to the process stands to be high. The prevailing attitude becomes less about whose students didn't do well on *X* and more about what the team can do collaboratively to ensure all of its students are becoming successful at *Y*.

It is worth noting that teachers continue to cover curricular content during these weeks. It's not as if everything stands still for three or four weeks while we fill student learning gaps identified in Data Meeting 3. What tends to be the situation in most schools is that while teachers implement strategic plans of action to correct learning gaps, business as usual marches on, and new lessons on new topics continue as before. Some schools designate a specific day of the week (or one every two weeks) to target efforts on older, yet unmastered topics. The team's action plan can take center stage on these days without interrupting the flow of new material covered during the rest of the week. Although this approach may seem to sacrifice a large chunk of instruction time, *not* incorporating opportunities for these efforts often turns out to be more costly.

Looking at Teacher Work

Looking at student and teacher work is a key part of what authentic PLCs do (Venables, 2011). It is worth pointing out, however, a distinction between the two. When teacher teams look at student work, they are looking at *after-the-fact* information and evidence. Student work is, by definition, work already produced by the students, so any action PLCs take regarding that work is reactive. In contrast, when teacher teams review lesson plans, teacher rubrics, teacher instructional strategies, and so forth, they are looking at teacher work that *precedes* student work. In this way, evaluating and revising teacher work is a *proactive* rather than a *reactive* endeavor. It makes sense for PLCs to spend at least as much time—arguably, more time—examining teacher work as student work because it has the power to affect student performance. Several protocols can help PLCs in critically examining teacher work.

The Tuning Protocol

The Tuning Protocol, developed by Joseph McDonald and Stephen Allen in the early 1990s, is one of the most useful and versatile tools used in education and is particularly well suited for examining teacher work. With this protocol, a teacher presents a lesson, an activity, or a rubric he or she is planning to use with students. The teacher team reviews the work presented and offers both warm (affirming) and cool (critical) feedback to the presenting teacher. The PLC members discuss which attributes of the teacher work they believe are worth keeping and also offer suggestions for how to make the teacher work better. The steps of the protocol look like this:

1. Introduction.
2. Presentation of student work and context.
3. Clarifying questions.
4. Examination of student work samples.
5. Pause for participants to think of warm and cool feedback they will offer.
6. Warm and cool feedback.
7. Reflection.
8. Debrief.

See pages 119–122 of the Appendix for a full overview of the protocol.

The Tuning Protocol is structured so that the teacher presenting the work speaks without interruption or discussion from the team. Similarly, while the team members discuss the work, the presenting teacher makes no comments or interjections. This structure may be a bit awkward for teacher teams experiencing it for the first time, but it promotes an unwavering focus on the presenting teacher's work and lessens the likelihood of defensiveness during the cool feedback.

The protocol also includes a segment during which the presenting teacher can reflect, aloud, on feedback he or she has received. Because this reflection occurs after feedback has been given in its entirety, and because the rest of the teacher team listens without speaking during the teacher's reflection, the tendency for the group to engage in critical/defensive back-and-forth banter is greatly reduced.

The following list illustrates examples of future work for which the Tuning Protocol is useful:

Assessment-Related Work

- Ungraded tests/quizzes
- Portfolio requirements
- Student projects
- Writing assignments
- Rubrics
- Computer-based assessments
- Lab reports

Instruction-Related Work

- Individual lessons (including technology-based lessons)
- Unit lessons
- Plans for lesson warm-ups
- Plans for lesson closure
- Instructional activities (including games)
- Plans for intervention
- Computer-based instruction

Classroom Procedures

- Homework policies
- Grading policies
- Procedures for grouping students
- Discipline policies
- Time management

The more collaborative a teacher team is in producing teacher work, the less likely it is that a teacher on the team will bring work that hasn't been co-created with the rest of the team. If the rest of the team *has* co-created the work, sharing warm and especially cool feedback is obviously more difficult. In the vast majority of PLCs I have worked with, however, much of the teacher work is planned collaboratively but includes activities and strategies that individual teachers implement. In those cases, the Tuning Protocol is well suited for offering valuable feedback to the owner of the individual work, even when much of the surrounding work was co-created by the team. Teams consisting of teachers of several grade levels or different subjects can get valuable feedback from one another because there are teachers on the team who had no hand in creating the work of a teacher or pair of teachers on the team.

Several other well-developed protocols for examining teacher (and student) work are described in *The Practice of Authentic PLCs* (Venables, 2011), *Protocols for Professional Learning* (Easton, 2009), and *The Power of Protocols* (McDonald et al., 2007).

The Planning Protocol Revisited

In the previous chapter on Data Meeting 4, we saw the usefulness of the Planning Protocol as the team created its Data Action Plan. Now, during implementation of that plan, that protocol will help the team again.

One of the benefits of having weekly PLC meetings during this four-week Implementation Period is that instructional approaches tried by the team that are not working in the classroom can be reviewed, revised, omitted, and replaced in real time. The team can use the rubric in the Planning Protocol as a guide to ensure high-quality revisions.

Looking at Student Work

As team members make modifications to their classroom instruction during the Implementation Period, students will be producing work that will reveal just how successful the teacher work is. No matter how refined, how well developed, or how scrutinized our teacher work is, if the resulting student work is of poor quality or demonstrates little understanding, then the teacher work was, in the end, ineffective. As a teacher team navigates the charted course toward its goal, reviewing student work as it is produced gives team members the opportunity to make steering adjustments along the way and stay the course. This source of formative data is a vital piece of the feedback loop: teachers plan → students produce → teachers plan, and so on.

When teacher teams look at student work, they do so for a variety of reasons. Sometimes they review the work to see how it aligns with a standard. Other times they use the student work to assess the degree to which the class has demonstrated mastery against a standard. They may participate in collaborative scoring of student work to calibrate and acquire a common notion for what constitutes quality work. At times, the teacher team uses the work formatively to retool its current instruction on a topic. The teacher team may also review student work to monitor the progress of individual students, of a whole class, or of subgroups of students. In all of these cases, student work is brought to the table and reviewed by the teacher team.

It is important to point out that the student work may or may not be graded assessments. Both classwork completed by students during instruction and homework are also valuable sources of information that teachers can use to understand how well students are mastering the standards. To encourage the PLC to have a structured, productive discussion about student work, two protocols are particularly useful.

Notice and Wonder Protocol for Student Work

During Data Meeting 1, we used the Notice and Wonder Protocol for our first crack at having a discussion around data (see the Appendix, pp. 114–115). With minor modifications, this protocol is equally useful for looking at student work.

Using the Notice and Wonder Protocol for looking at student work functions essentially the same way it did for initially reviewing data: teachers offer observations in the way of Notice Statements in the first round and then offer more probing Wonder Statements in the second round. It is often telling to hear the factual, objective observations teachers make during Round 1, because they define the things that are important to them. For example, consider an 8th grade English language arts PLC looking at a piece of student writing. If the majority of team members make Notice Statements about the mechanics of the writing rather than the argument the student makes in the writing, then it would suggest that the team collectively values that particular component of their students' writing.

Another advantage for teams engaging in Notice Statements is that the process itself is an exercise in separating the work (student work) from the person (the teacher in whose class the work was produced). By simply "noticing" factual characteristics of the work, the team's comments are generally (although not always) void of judgment, evaluation, or inference, which lessens the defensiveness of the teacher whose student created the work. It's hard to argue with "I noticed that four of the five paragraphs written by the student contain fewer than three sentences."

A final cautionary note regarding Notice Statements: it is important for teacher teams to notice characteristics present in the work and not those missing from the work. Otherwise, the team may begin to delineate all the characteristics they think *ought* to be present but are not, and the focus shifts toward suggestions and away from observations. When this happens, the safety of the presenting teacher in hearing only factual statements quickly erodes as the team becomes more evaluative and prescriptive. A presenting teacher is more likely to become defensive if Notice Statements point out what's missing rather than simply state what exists in the work.

In Round 2 of the Notice and Wonder Protocol, the team offers Wonder Statements about the student work. These statements tend to be of four types: *I wonder why, I wonder if, I wonder how,* and *I wonder whether.* The timbre of the team's comments is inquisitive. Wonder Statements can be inquiries of curiosity, suggestion, feedback, and alternative perspective.

Since developing the Notice and Wonder Protocol a few years ago, I have modified it in one significant way. The original version (Venables, 2011) did not include a segment for team members to openly discuss one another's Notice and Wonder Statements. Instead, these statements originally were offered during their respective rounds and not discussed as a group. There was and remains a good reason for that: if open discussion is permitted after each Notice or Wonder Statement, the team's focus can easily get derailed, and the time required to complete the protocol increases substantially.

Nevertheless, teams would often ask me, "But when are teachers permitted to discuss what they are hearing, what their teammates are sharing?" To address this concern, I have modified the original Notice and Wonder Protocol to permit the team facilitator/coach (only) to respond to any Wonder Statement. This exception to the no-discussion clause in the original protocol applies to Wonder Statements only—Notice Statements are still shared without discussion, as specified in the original protocol. In addition, only the coach should initiate a response to a teacher's Wonder Statement.

The coach's response, if there is one, should immediately follow the Wonder Statement and generally take the form of a question directed either to the teacher sharing the Wonder Statement ("Can you say more about that?") or to the PLC as a whole ("I'd like to hear someone respond to what Ms. Evans has just shared."). With only the facilitator responding to the Wonder Statements, the discussion that follows is likely to be brief but substantive, and to maintain focus on the work in question. A skillful coach can use his or her responses to push the ideas deeper, help clarify points of confusion, or steer the team's thinking to areas of concern that are, at least in the coach's mind, most likely to lead to improved instruction. Here are some possible responses a PLC coach might have to a teacher's Wonder Statement:

- Could you say more about that?
- I'd like to hear someone respond to that.
- Who owns that?
- How could that Wonder Statement guide us?
- What if . . . ?
- How does that square with our Planning Protocol rubric?
- What assumptions are you/we making about . . . ?
- What does that Wonder Statement say about our practice?
- What kinds of issues are bubbling to the surface?
- Why should we care about . . . ?
- Does anyone else wonder that?
- So how *would* we . . . ?
- How would we know?
- How is that different from . . . ?
- If we were to do . . . , what might result?

- Should we know the answer to that?
- Why do we . . . ?
- Who says . . . is best?
- What are you/we *really* wondering about here?
- How would you/we bring . . . into the classroom?

It is worth noting that the PLC coach should not feel compelled to respond to all the Wonder Statements; indeed, responding to only those few statements that open up opportunities for the team to think more expansively about the work and their own practice is preferable to asking a large number of questions. As is the case with many pursuits of authentic PLCs, these judgment calls rest with a qualified facilitator who leads the team and who trusts his or her own instincts in seizing growth moments with the team.

The Tuning Protocol for Student Work

The Tuning Protocol is not only an effective tool to use in discussing teacher work; it may also be used to look at student work. During the Implementation Period between Data Meetings 4 and 5, the Tuning Protocol can offer teachers on the team the chance to receive warm and cool feedback about their students' work. Compared with the Notice and Wonder Protocol, the feedback offered during the Tuning Protocol can be both more pointed and more affirming. It is often accompanied by more suggestions for improvement. Depending on the nature of the student work and the readiness of the teacher to hear warm and cool feedback, the Tuning Protocol is often the best choice for reviewing student work. The segment in the protocol that has the presenting teacher share reflections on the feedback is particularly poignant; it forces an acknowledgment on the teacher's part that some things should be changed. While this reflection may be tacitly included in the Notice and Wonder Protocol, it is more deliberate—and therefore often more effective—in the Tuning Protocol.

Whether reviewing teacher or student work, the PLC coach should meet with the presenting teacher outside regular meeting times to decide together which protocol would work best for the work to be presented. If the PLC coach does not have this one-on-one conversation with the presenting teacher, the teacher may not be completely on board with the protocol selected and may become defensive in responding to feedback.

Overcoming Obstacles to Implementation

Perhaps by definition, the Implementation Period between Data Meetings 4 and 5 is full of novel ways of doing things: new strategies during classroom instruction, new assessment approaches, new lessons on old topics, and even new uses of existing technologies. It is this change happening in the classroom that is the nexus of improved student learning. However, new ways of doing things beget new ways of messing up and running up against previously nonexistent obstacles. In this section, we'll look at some useful protocols for helping teachers resolve issues related to their instruction—particularly the newer aspects of their practice that are typical during the Implementation Period.

The Consultancy Protocol

The Consultancy Protocol was developed by educators affiliated with the National School Reform Faculty (NSRF) for the purpose of helping teachers work through dilemmas or issues pertaining to their practice that have no obvious solution. The dilemmas that work best with the Consultancy Protocol are those

- That are not already on their way to being solved;
- Whose solution does not require other people to change their behavior;
- For which previous solution strategies may have been tried and failed; and
- That may be causing secondary issues/dilemmas.

The steps of the protocol are as follows (see pp. 123–129 of the Appendix for a full overview):

1. The presenter gives an overview of the dilemma he or she is struggling with and frames a question for the Consultancy group to consider.
2. The Consultancy group asks the presenter clarifying (factual) questions about the dilemma.
3. The Consultancy group asks the presenter probing (analytical) questions about the dilemma.
4. Consultancy group members discuss the dilemma with one another.
5. The presenter shares with the group reflections on what he or she has heard and is now thinking.
6. The facilitator leads a brief conversation about the group's observation of the Consultancy process.

The Consultancy process pushes teachers to think more deeply about the dilemmas and about their assumptions surrounding the issues that may be impeding success at solving them. In addition to pushing the presenting teacher's thinking, the PLC commonly offers suggestions for things the teacher may try to address the situation. It is perfectly all right if the Consultancy Protocol does not culminate with a firm solution for the presenting teacher; it is more important that the presenting teacher view the issue more deeply and in new ways, think about possible options for moving forward, and arrive at a plan for resolution at some point, often days after going through the protocol.

Clarifying and Probing Questions

During the Consultancy Protocol, the teacher team asks clarifying questions of the presenting teacher—the teacher who owns the dilemma. *Clarifying* questions are asked for the benefit of the team member who asks them, and their aim is to elicit more information pertaining to the context surrounding the dilemma. The presenting teacher's responses to clarifying questions tend to be brief and factual. For example, a teacher on the team might ask, "Are you noticing a similar behavior with the other students in the class?", to which the presenting teacher may reply, "No, not really, and it really only happens when I put this student in groups." The point of clarifying questions is to provide more information pertinent to the dilemma that the presenting teacher may have missed when he or she presented it.

If the presenting teacher needs to pause for any length of time after being asked a clarifying question, the question is most likely not a clarifying question but rather a *probing* question. Probing questions are asked for the benefit of the presenting teacher; their aim is to help the presenting teacher think more expansively about the dilemma. The presenting teacher's beliefs, assumptions, and values often bubble to the surface while he or she ponders a response to the probing question. Often, the presenting teacher was not previously aware of these beliefs, assumptions, and values, and their revelation is largely the point of asking probing questions. We don't ask probing questions to evaluate or in any way judge the presenting teacher's dilemma or attempts at solving the dilemma; we ask them to help push the presenting teacher's thinking about the matter in new ways, from new perspectives. The solution to the dilemma often lies therein.

Asking good probing questions is an acquired skill. They require deeper thinking on the part of both the team members asking the questions and the presenting teachers answering them. They are the kinds of questions therapists are good at asking—not judgmental or prescriptive, but useful for getting the client to think more expansively about an issue. In contrast, clarifying questions are the kinds of questions a newspaper reporter might ask in pursuing the basic facts of a story.

Probing questions are not disguised suggestions or leading questions. The Consultancy Protocol includes a specific segment (Step 4) when the teacher team members discuss the dilemma among themselves and make suggestions to remedy the issue. Suggestions are best left to this segment of the protocol. When team members embed suggestions in probing questions (e.g., "What would happen if you put the students in groups for homework corrections?"), the effect can be off-putting to the presenting teacher. If teachers have useful suggestions for the presenting teacher, those suggestions should be offered during the discussion segment and not thinly veiled as questions. The line between a good probing question and a suggestion masquerading as a question can be blurry at times, so keep this rule of thumb in mind to make the distinction clear: if the asking teacher has in mind the "correct" answer to the question, then it is probably not a probing question.

For more guidance in asking probing questions, see the School Reform Initiative's *Pocket Guide to Asking Probing Questions* (http://schoolreforminitiative.org/doc/probing_questions_guide.pdf) and "PLC Coach's Guide to Asking Deeper Questions" (see the Appendix, pp. 130–132).

The Shared Dilemma Protocol

The Consultancy Protocol is nicely suited for helping teachers in the PLC address a challenging issue or dilemma. But what if the issue or dilemma is owned by *all* members of the PLC? To be sure, the greater the extent to which PLC members are collaborating both in and out of the classroom, the greater the chance of each teacher on the team hitting an obstacle or facing a dilemma that is common to all teachers on the team. To deal with these instances, my friend and colleague Cari Begin and I have developed the Shared Dilemma Protocol (see the Appendix, pp. 133–134).

The Shared Dilemma Protocol works in a similar manner to that of the Consultancy Protocol in that all participating teachers are attempting to gain insight into the dilemma and find a solution. In Step 1, the team succinctly articulates the dilemma and records it on chart paper or in a collaborative Google Drive document. Often, the mere act of putting words to the issue helps the team gain insights it may not have had previously. Members of the PLC who aren't aware of particular aspects of the shared dilemma may ask clarifying questions during this step.

In Step 2, each team member notes and asks probing questions of the group, although there is no attempt to answer these questions until all the probing questions have been shared. In the next few steps, the team discusses big ideas or themes that revealed themselves during the probing question step, and the teachers use these ideas to generate possible solutions. Because the Shared Dilemma Protocol keeps the discussion focused on the issue and its possible solutions, it is a useful tool in helping teams find a way to overcome a common obstacle.

Looking at Text

Of all the tasks I witness PLCs doing together, few impress me more than a team of teachers engaged in a text-based discussion related to some aspect of their practice. It goes to the very heart of what it means to be a professional and what it means to be part of an authentic professional *learning* community. It is invigorating to hold such a discussion and a real treat to watch one.

Having text-based discussions is an ideal way for teacher teams to gain new knowledge about some aspect of their teaching and to construct community meaning of this new knowledge. Whether team members have read a chapter in Carol Ann Tomlinson's *How to Differentiate Instruction in Mixed-Ability Classrooms* (2004), an article on the flipped classroom from ASCD's digital newsletter *SmartBrief,* or an essay on motivating students in *Educational Leadership,* the discussion that ensues results in new learning by the team as a whole and by the individuals who make up the team.

As follow-up to the discussion, teachers try new strategies in their classrooms during this Implementation Period and assess their effectiveness in a subsequent meeting. In these ways, looking at text stands to be a hugely beneficial use of PLC meeting time. Sadly, with the frenetic pace of most schools and the push for teacher teams to do so many other things (several of which do not affect student learning), text-related discussions are all too seldom practiced.

For teacher teams wishing to engage in professional reading and team discussion of that reading, I recommend three particularly well-suited protocols to keep the conversation focused and substantive. Each protocol assumes that teachers have read the text before the meeting and have highlighted and annotated it as they would any piece of text from which they are learning. What follows is a brief description of how each one works and in what ways the team might utilize it. The full protocols are available in the Appendix.

Text-Based Seminar

Developed by Gene Thompson-Grove of the School Reform Initiative, this protocol allows teachers on the team to comment freely on individual passages from the text, provided they adhere to the following guidelines:

1. Refer to the text and challenge others to go to the text.
2. Listen actively.
3. Build on what others say, referring to them by name.
4. Don't step on others' talk. Allow for silences and pauses; make time and space so everyone can participate.
5. Converse directly with one another, and let the conversation flow as much as possible without raising hands or using a speaker's list.
6. Make the assumptions underlying your comments explicit to others.
7. Ask questions of others in order to build understanding.

In addition to these guidelines, I suggest two more guidelines for the PLCs I work with:

8. Watch your airtime.
9. Refrain from autobiographical litanies.

Of course, we want teachers to connect the text to themselves and vice versa. Guideline 9 helps teachers to steer away from being too focused on what they do and instead to focus more on the text. Brief autobiographical comments are welcome; lengthy memoirs are not. The team may benefit from hearing how a teacher connects the text to his or her practice, but teams are generally less interested in detailed reports about what an individual teacher does.

Four *A*s Text Protocol

In this protocol developed by Judith Gray, teachers on the team read the text (or reread their highlights of the text) and individually write down four *A*s from the text, including

- Something they think is an *assumption* of the author.
- A part of the text they *agree* with.
- A part of the text they want to *argue* with.
- An aspect of the text they *aspire* to.

Each teacher shares his or her four *A*s, and the team then discusses their implications for students in the classroom. This protocol is particularly effective with PLCs whose members are reluctant to embrace the work of the PLC. These team members can probably find something in the text they disagree with and are usually quite happy to share it.

The Final Word Protocol

In this protocol, each teacher selects a passage from the text that holds some personal meaning for him or her, whether that means the teacher was able to relate to it, agreed with it, or took issue with it. The first teacher to go reads his or her selected passage without commenting; then each teacher on the team remarks on the passage until the floor is again granted to the first teacher, who responds to the remarks about his or her chosen passage and has the "final word" on it. This process continues until all teachers have had an opportunity to read their selected passages.

Each of these three text-driven protocols can be an effective way to encourage new learning and meaningful, focused discussion among the teachers on the team. As PLCs try out these protocols, they will come to like some better than others and gain insight about which protocol is the best fit for any given piece of text. Most important, teachers can gain new perspectives or learn new strategies that they can test in their classrooms during the Implementation Period of the Data Action Model.

From the Trenches

School: Hartman Middle School (HMS)
Location: Blueville-Florence, Colorado
Grades: 6–8
Demographics: Large, suburban, high-SES
Students: 91 percent white, 9 percent students of color, 0 percent eligible for free or reduced lunch
PLC: Grade 8, math, five teachers

HMS is in its fourth year of having PLCs. Teacher collaboration is highly valued by principal Joan Coates, and that has had a trickle-down effect to the teaching staff. The math PLCs at all three grade levels were originally the most reluctant of the teams to embrace PLCs, but by now, most team members have settled into the school's collaborative culture.

The school's transition to the Common Core has helped build this sense of collegiality. The Standards for Mathematical Practice were demanding on teachers, and they turned to one another to make sense of them. These new standards challenged business as usual, and suddenly teachers had a reason to change the way they had always done things. This became a perfect example of authenticity in a PLC: teachers collaborating in meaningful ways for meaningful reasons, not just meeting to collaborate for collaboration's sake. As they constructed community knowledge together about what the standards were saying, they grew stronger as a team and more interdependent.

The Grade 8 Math PLC is facilitated by Erv Thompson, who helped the team work through this process. He was trained as a coach at a Grapple Institute he attended two years ago. His style is a bit rigid, and he goes strictly "by the book" when it comes to leading protocols or discussions. The team members accept his approach and have learned to work well together under his leadership. Three of the five 8th grade math teachers teach Algebra 1 in addition to Math 8, and Mr. Thompson also teaches a section of geometry to advanced students. Because all of the teachers teach at least one class of Math 8, they derived their Target Learning Goal from this curriculum and based it on gaps they had identified from the data in previous meetings. The gaps the team decided to focus on all stemmed from students' difficulty with applications of linear functions.

Now in their Implementation Period, the teachers have been trying the instructional tactics listed in their action plan in their classrooms. When they meet each week, they bring student work to share and analyze. Because not every Math 8 class is in the same place on any given day, teachers who have tried certain strategies from the team's action plan share how things went for them at the start of PLC meetings. This discussion clearly benefits the rest of the team.

From the Trenches *(continued)*

As part of their action plan, the team members earmarked Friday as the day they would temporarily suspend current topics and carry out various components of their plan to meet their Target Learning Goal. Their agendas varied from Friday to Friday: sometimes they would try out new lessons or activities that they had agreed to in their action plan; other times, they would start with one-problem quizzes and discuss them immediately after students took them. Sometimes the students worked in groups or at solution stations on previously assigned problems. All these strategies were gleaned from the Strategies Search the teachers conducted during previous data meetings.

The PLC members regularly brought samples of student and teacher work to their meetings during the four-week Implementation Period. Informally but thoroughly, the team analyzed the work through the lens of how it stacked up against the Target Learning Goal. For one of the meetings during the Implementation Period, the team tried out the Shared Dilemma Protocol under Mr. Thompson's leadership. Their dilemma for the protocol homed in on two of the Common Core State Standards for Mathematical Practice as they applied to the study of linear functions. At the conclusion of that meeting, several of the teachers commented on the meeting's usefulness. As the team members continued to see progress in their students' learning, their sense of purpose in the work and interdependence as a team increased.

Data Meeting 5

Evaluating Success and Determining Next Steps

NOTICE

WONDER

ASK

BRING

TRACK

IDENTIFY

SET

SEARCH

DEVELOP

IMPLEMENT

EVALUATE

By the time of Data Meeting 5, a great deal of work has been done. In addition to the work completed at each of the previous four data meetings, the team has been implementing various aspects of its Data Action Plan; convening once a week, often with artifacts from those instructional endeavors; and briefing one another about what has been successful and what still needs improvement in pursuing the Target Learning Goal. All this has been happening while business as usual continues: teachers are presenting new material to their students and covering new standards while they also work to address students' learning gaps of previously covered material. It is important that teams acknowledge this confluence of instructional activity. The curriculum and the instruction that supports students' learning of that curriculum do not stand still while learning gaps are filled. For this reason, many teams designate a particular day of the week to focus primarily on gaps related to previous content while they instruct students in new content on other days of the week.

Do First: Evaluate the Effectiveness of Implementation

The hour-long Data Meeting 5 is earmarked for team members to evaluate the extent to which they reached their Target Learning Goal and decide what to do next. In Data Meeting 3, the team had decided what it would accept as evidence that the goal was reached. Now, after a lengthy Implementation Period of specific instructional tactics laid out in the Data Action Plan, team members have amassed enough evidence to objectively judge the success of their action plan and determine whether they have met their

Target Learning Goal. Data Meeting 5 provides the time and focus to decide just that. For example, to cite an example of a SMART goal given in Data Meeting 3 (p. 52), have at least 80 percent of 4th grade students scored a 3 or 4 on the Writing Rubric dimension "Citing Evidence from Text"? Based on the pertinent artifacts—in this case, student writing samples—the team is able to assess whether this goal has been realized.

This process does not need to be done with statistical precision. The teacher team can review a stack of representative writing samples and answer the questions "Have we reached our goal? Or are these student papers lacking?" It's OK if teams are a bit more scientific in their approach to evaluating goal success, but in my experience, most teams are able to go through a dozen or so papers and make a judgment call based on what they see. This is the reality in most schools. Many PLCs are not willing to calculate percentages to decide whether they have met their goals.

Do Second: Decide on the Next Course of Action

Before deciding on the next course of action, the team must answer two straightforward questions:

- Do the student learning gaps persist?
- Are the students performing significantly better (in the areas identified) or not?

Because of its specificity, the Target Learning Goal defines "significantly" in this context. Depending on its answers to these two questions, the team can decide on its next course of action. The flowchart in Figure 11 illustrates the team's possible next steps.

Next Steps If the Learning Goal Was Met

There is a good chance that the team met its Target Learning Goal. Team members have been monitoring their success during the Implementation Period and have continued to meet during this time to alter their plan, if necessary, to ensure success.

— Figure 11 —

Flowchart to Determine Next Course of Action

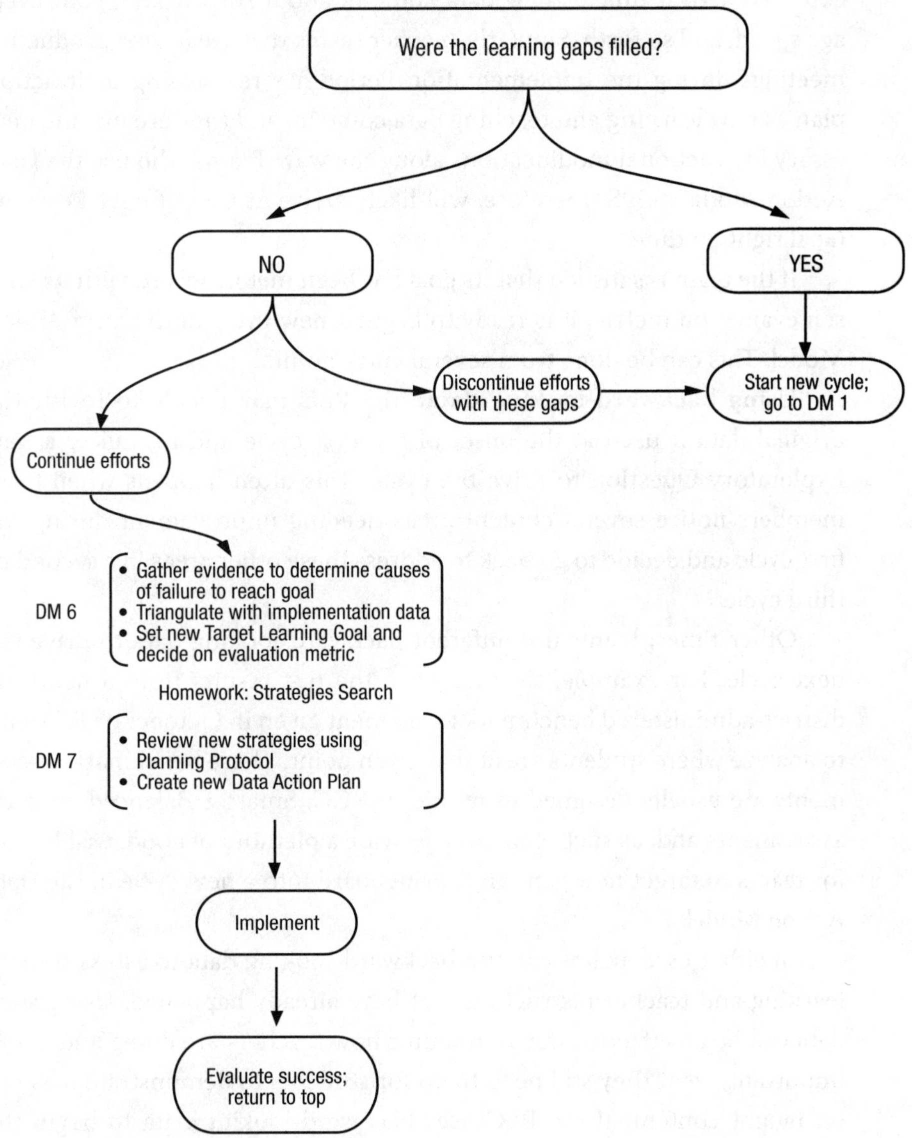

Think of the GPS app on your smartphone or in your car. It tells you what time you can expect to arrive at your destination. This arrival time is, in the end, always correct because the unit continually updates the expected arrival time as new data come in about road delays, your average speed, and so forth. Similarly, teacher teams that are having productive meetings during the Implementation Period are reassessing their action plan as new learning and teaching data come in, and they are making necessary instructional modifications along the way. Teams who use the Data Action Model's GPS, therefore, will likely arrive at their Target Learning Goal right on time.

If the team is satisfied that its goal has been met in accord with its chosen evaluation metric, it is ready to begin a new cycle in the Data Action Model. This can be done from several entry points.

Using backward-looking data. The PLC may decide to revisit the original data it used at the onset of the first cycle and formulate a new Exploratory Question to drive the cycle. This often happens when team members notice several content areas needing improvement during the first cycle and decide to go back to address these other areas in a second or third cycle.

Other times, teams use different backward-looking data to drive the next cycle. For example, they may use the test results from a quarterly district-administered benchmark assessment given in October or February to analyze where students are at that given point. These benchmark assessments are usually designed to mimic PARCC, Smarter Balanced, or state assessments and, as such, generally provide a plethora of good, usable data for teams to target new gaps and springboard into a new cycle in the Data Action Model.

In either case, teams can use backward-looking data to assess student learning and teacher instruction that have already happened. Using such data can be an effective way to monitor how teachers are doing and, more important, what they still need to do for students to demonstrate mastery on taught content. If the PLC uses backward-looking data to begin the next cycle, it will proceed much as it did before: review the data (using the

Notice and Wonder Protocol), generate an Exploratory Question, triangulate the data, identify learning and instructional gaps, set a goal, develop an action plan, implement the plan, and evaluate its success.

Using forward-looking data. Not all PLCs use backward-looking data to kick off a second cycle of the Data Action Model. For example, a PLC may not refer back to the data it used in August, say, to start its first cycle; because these data often reflect the performances of previous cohorts of students (as in the case of end-of-course or CCSS assessment data), the data may no longer be very useful. For this reason, teacher teams frequently opt to administer pre-tests to their students before a particular unit of study has begun. Teachers get valuable information in this way about what students already know—and don't know—about an impending topic. For items students missed on the pre-test, the PLC will have to decide whether this performance is due to the fact that students have not yet studied the topic or that they lack skills they should have learned in previous units of study or grade levels.

If the team uses forward-looking data from pre-tests to begin the next cycle, it will identify student gaps from these data without needing to generate an Exploratory Question or triangulate the pre-test assessment data. Because the Data Action Model is truncated with forward-looking data, the team's next steps after identifying student gaps are for teachers to individually conduct a Strategies Search between data meetings and proceed as a team from that point much as it did the first time. See the discussion on page 109 in Putting It All Together, as well as Figure 12 (p. 111), for further insight on this truncated process.

Next Steps If the Learning Goal Was Not Met

Although there is a good chance that the Target Learning Goal has been met, it sometimes happens that the answers to the essential questions posed on page 94 are *yes* and *no,* respectively; that is, gaps *do* persist, and student achievement on the topic is *not* significantly better. In this case, the team members must make a critical decision. They must choose either (1) to discontinue their efforts to fill these gaps and direct their efforts to addressing new gaps or (2) to continue to try to fill these gaps. If the PLC members decide on the first option, they will proceed much as they would if the Target Learning Goal had been reached: by beginning a new data cycle (see the section "Next Steps If the Learning Goal Was Met").

If the team persists in attempting to fill the learning gaps, it will need to hold two additional data meetings and do some homework between them.

Data Meeting 6: Determining the causes of not reaching the goal. Several reasons may explain why the goal was missed and the gaps remain. Perhaps the goal itself was too ambitious, or the team members didn't monitor their progress enough during the Implementation Period, or the strategies selected for their action plan were ineffective. It could be that the team's evaluation metric or post-test was too demanding or not valid. The teachers on the team may have gravitated to their original teaching methods instead of actually implementing the instructional tactics that the team agreed to in its Data Action Plan. The cause or causes of the missed goal will dictate the team's actions. For this reason, Data Meeting 6 is dedicated to gathering evidence to determine precisely why the goal was not met, triangulating the available implementation data, and using these artifacts to set a new goal and possibly determine a new metric for evaluation (although the team may decide to use the same evaluation metric again).

Because the content and basic process are the same and therefore familiar to the teachers on the team, they can generally achieve all of these tasks in a single data meeting. Data Meeting 6 ends with a reminder by the PLC coach for the teachers to research one or two new activities or strategies and prepare to share them at the next meeting. This homework is essentially a new Strategies Search on the same standard or topic in question.

Data Meeting 7: Constructing a new action plan. A final data meeting is required to review and score the strategies and activities the teachers share. Just as before, the team members use the rubric from the Planning Protocol to score each activity or lesson component. After this discussion, the team decides which activities will be put to use and creates a new Data Action Plan using the Action Plan Tracking Sheet.

After Data Meetings 6 and 7 have occurred, the team begins a second Implementation Period in the classroom using the new ideas. This stage may be shorter this time around for a variety of reasons, but it is structured the same as before: implement → meet to discuss → alter tactics as needed → implement → meet to discuss, and so on. Teachers continue to bring and review goal-related student work to each PLC meeting during this time.

Once the teachers implement each of the instructional tactics listed in their action plan, they spend a part of the very next scheduled PLC meeting using the evaluation metric to gauge the success of their efforts. If they decide that they have met their goal this time, they begin a new cycle of the Data Action Model. If they failed to meet their goal a second time (which is extremely rare), they again must decide whether they wish to continue their efforts to eradicate the student learning gaps in question.

In the next and final chapter, we'll look at overarching considerations in using the Data Action Model, such as the roles of the PLC and the administration and the time line for using the model.

Putting It All Together

The Role of the PLC

At this point, the reader should be clear on how essential I believe the PLC or teacher team is in seeing the Data Action Model to successful fruition. Nearly everything in the model happens in the context of teachers working together as a team. Whether it is looking at data, bringing new data to the table, reviewing artifacts, setting a goal, or creating an action plan to reach that goal, it is the teacher team that collectively and collaboratively pursues these tasks. Fading fast are the days when teachers might have tried to do anything remotely akin to this process by themselves. To do this complex, time-consuming, and important work, a team is not just preferred; it is essential.

Richard DuFour, author of numerous books and articles on PLCs, reminds us that the question we should be asking is not "Are teachers collaborating?" but rather "What are they collaborating about?" (DuFour et al., 2006). The Data Action Model, when followed with fidelity, impels teacher teams to collaborate about the "right stuff." What could be more important than collaborating on identifying our students' learning gaps and deciding on plans of action to correct them?

In my experience, every high-functioning PLC is led by a high-functioning facilitator. To be sure, not every model of professional learning communities in the literature insists on well-trained PLC facilitators as I do, and my approach differs in this way from those of DuFour and others (DuFour et al., 2006; Hord & Sommers, 2008; Venables, 2011). In my experience working directly with scores of PLCs, those that flourish and achieve high results for themselves and for their students are almost without exception led by well-trained coaches. The road to success can often be bumpy, winding, and uphill. Without guidance from a skilled teacher to facilitate this important work, even the best-intentioned teams often flounder. When team members don't have a coach to keep them focused and push them to ask the hard questions of themselves and one another, they can consume large amounts of time weaving in and out of focus as they limp along, trying to do their best for their students. The team may eventually arrive at positive results using this undisciplined approach, but the process doesn't need to be that murky, and success doesn't need to take that long. When it comes to helping PLCs use their time efficiently and effectively, I cannot imagine doing this important work without the guidance of a trained and skillful PLC coach.

Vertical Teams

Some elementary and middle school PLCs include teachers who teach different grade levels. In such schools, PLCs tend to be subject-specific—for example, a math PLC composed of 6th, 7th, and 8th grade teachers. This arrangement is not uncommon in small schools that may have a single math teacher for each grade level. In small elementary schools, each PLC may encompass several grade levels (e.g., a K–1 team, a 2–3 team, and a 4–5 team). Many urban schools, once very large, have split to form several small schools in order to increase their effectiveness. Although the potential benefits of these smaller schools are clear, this new configuration sometimes results in a propagation of PLCs consisting of teachers of multiple grade levels because there are not enough teachers teaching individual grades in any one school to form single-grade teacher teams.

These types of multi-grade-level teams are known as *vertical teams.* Although vertical teams have advantages over horizontal (i.e., same-grade-level) teams when it comes to looking at a progression of topics across grade levels, reviewing data in vertical teams can be tricky. For example, a middle school English language arts PLC that includes two teachers from each grade level taught at the school (6–8) must acknowledge that it has three distinct data sets to consider in any data conversation. This situation is not ideal, to be sure, but the team can still use the Data Action Model as a tool to improve practice.

For example, the team may decide to spotlight a single grade level's data in a particular cycle, rotating through the others in subsequent cycles. Doing so does not imply that the pairs of teachers in the other two grade levels are not doing similar work with their own data, just that the team as a larger group, during meetings, would focus on one grade's pair of teachers at a time. For PLCs taking this approach, some meeting times would likely splinter out, with the three pairs working separately for part (or all) of the meeting and later coming together to report out to the team as a whole.

In addition to the advantage of having a firsthand sense of how particular standards progress through the grade levels, another benefit of the vertical team is that there is considerable opportunity for valuable feedback from teammates when they do not own the work. For example, when the 7th grade teachers in a 6–8 ELA PLC share their Exploratory Question with the rest of the team, they get useful feedback from the other four teachers that they would not get if all six teachers had discussed and arrived at the Exploratory Question together. Other steps in the Data Action Model would work similarly, with teachers in the subgroups (pairs) of the vertical team working together and then joining the other pairs to share and receive feedback.

The Role of the Administration

Like managers in the business sector, school principals often focus on results. This mind-set is especially true in the post–No Child Left Behind, high-stakes assessment world in which educators reside today. With assessments come data, and with the Data Action Model for teachers and teacher teams to use in reviewing and responding to the data, the results that principals want to see are more likely to happen, especially when principals support teacher teams in general and use of the model specifically. In working with schools to develop and maintain high-functioning PLCs, I generally suggest that each member of the school's administrative team join at least one PLC at the school and attend meetings consistently. In this way, the administration sends a clear message that the work of the PLC is important, and, by attending meetings and contributing during team discussions, the administrator can help encourage deep discussions.

That said, it is also important for administrators to monitor themselves so that they do not take over discussions, dominate airtime, or supplant the role of the PLC coach, who is the rightful facilitator of the team. A good rule of thumb is that the administrative member of the PLC should contribute about as often as the least-contributing member of the group. Erring on the side of too few comments is substantially better than erring on the side of too many—even if administrators have a worthy opinion or thoughtful comment. The teachers in the PLC need to become *interdependent* and not depend on the administrator to do all of the hard thinking, settle debates, or guide decision making.

In addition to supporting PLCs through their presence at team meetings, principals can support teams' efforts to review and respond to data and make that work a priority in their schools through the allocation of time and resources. Teacher teams are often more productive when meetings are held during the school day rather than after school. When daily schedules are structured so that teachers have common planning times (a practice that has become fairly common nowadays), principals are supporting the work of the teams.

The work of the team is also more effective—and more often realizes the results that principals are looking for—when the PLC coach has been sufficiently trained to facilitate the team's data work. The principal must allocate sufficient professional development funding to make this training possible.

Principals can also support teacher teams by requiring them to produce evidence of their successes in the way of student and teacher data artifacts. In New York City, where I have indirectly worked with six schools during the last two years, teacher teams use a large Google spreadsheet to keep track of each step as they proceed through the Data Action Model. Principals at these schools may access these spreadsheets at any time, and they are continually kept abreast of the progress and quality of the teams' work. In states like Georgia, where work with PLCs has become part of the statewide teacher evaluation system, these kinds of documents act as evidence for teacher and school evaluation purposes.

Time Line for the Data Action Model

There is no one-size-fits-all template for using the Data Action Model because schools have access to different kinds of data and have different schedules as to when the data arrive. That being the case, most schools that have used the Data Action Model successfully have started their first cycle at the beginning of the school year. In general, the first cycle takes up to nine weeks, spanning the first quarter of the school year, and teams use end-of-course or CCSS assessment data to begin their inquiry.

A second cycle generally begins at the start of the second quarter or marking period, and teams might use the same data (and pursue a new Exploratory Question) or use different data, possibly from district benchmark assessments. Many districts administer one or two benchmark assessments yearly, and if they use two, one is often administered to students during each of the second and third quarters. These benchmark assessments are intended to reflect where students are in their mastery of course standards so that administrators and teachers can take action to fill learning gaps before it's too late. For this reason, benchmark assessments are typically a good source of data for use in the Data Action Model, especially for topics already taught but not adequately mastered by students (as opposed to missed items on the benchmark assessments that represent topics of future instruction).

In districts that don't administer benchmark assessments, teacher teams can use their own semicumulative assessments (e.g., midterm exams for middle and high schools) to gauge their students' progress and use the Data Action Model to respond to it. Teams can also use unit pre- and posttests, as suggested previously (see Data Meeting 5).

As a final note regarding the time line, when I visit a school or district using the Data Action Model, we decide together, with the administration and PLC coaches, which data we should use, how often to implement a new cycle, and how long the cycles should be, generally planning for the entire school year. We typically decide on these points when all PLC members return to school in August or September. This approach serves the purpose of getting all stakeholders on the same page and making it clear that there will be follow-up to everything set forth at the start of the school year. Each school is different and must decide these matters as it implements the model.

Three Commonly Asked Questions

In the time since I first developed the Data Action Model and trained school teams to use it, PLCs' implementation of the model has taught me a lot about what works best. In fact, from each school I have worked with, I have learned almost as much as the teachers being trained did. When I begin working with a school, I am usually asked a number of questions. In this final section, I share the three most common ones, and their answers.

How big should the goal be in any one cycle?

The goal—and therefore the size of the goal—is a direct result of the learning gaps identified by a team. This is why in Data Meeting 3, we not only pinpoint learning gaps but also rate them in terms of their prominence and significance. Once the team settles on which gap or gaps it would like to remedy, the goal follows in turn.

So, perhaps a better way of framing this question might be, "How big should the *gaps* be that we wish to fix?" To wind up with a goal that is too granular and then spend hours of meeting time working on it doesn't make a lot of sense. Going with a goal that encompasses several standards or a standard that recurs each quarter is more desirable than choosing a goal that is trivial or short-sighted by comparison. Often, particularly with ELA teams, the goal chosen reflects a standard that is woven throughout the school year, such as drawing inferences from text, or a goal related to nonfiction writing. These are not standards that are addressed once and then put to rest; students continue to develop these skills as they apply them throughout the school year with texts of various types and levels of complexity. Such crucial building-block skills make for useful Target Learning Goals to home in on.

Our PLC has difficulty going deep enough in our data discussions. As coach of the team, what can I do to push deeper thinking?

The first thing to do is to realize that although having relatively shallow data discussions is not desirable, it is also not uncommon, especially for teams beginning their work together or going through their first or second cycle of the Data Action Model.

A host of reasons explains why data discussions can fail to be substantive, productive, or useful in leading to impactful change in the classroom. Sometimes teacher teams focus blame on the students; sometimes teams rush to solve problems after taking only a brief and cursory look at the data; and sometimes teams arrive at secondary or trivial instructional causes of identified learning gaps and fail to address root causes of what the data are showing. To address these and other reasons behind wayward or unsubstantial data discussions, see "10 Potential Data Discussion Pitfalls" in the Appendix (p. 141), which suggests strategies that coaches can use to help their teams go deeper.

If we use pre-test data to launch the second (or a subsequent) cycle of the Data Action Model, how do we approach the triangulation step?

You can't—at least not in the usual place in the cycle, which comes after deciding an Exploratory Question and before identifying gaps.

Pre-test data are *forward-looking* data (see Data Meeting 5 for more information on using forward-looking and backward-looking data). That is, pre-tests reflect content that has not yet been taught (at least during the current school year). For this reason, no artifacts would be available for the team to use during the triangulation step to figure out more about what is happening and what has contributed to the learning gaps detected.

Pre-tests are diagnostic and are particularly useful in showing what students already know about an impending topic. They are less useful in providing information on why students didn't do well on certain topic items. Did students miss the items because they have never seen the content before? Did the items assume prerequisite skills that the students have not mastered? Were students exposed to the topic last year, but they didn't retain the pertinent content? It's hard to say from the pre-test results. Without going back and finding out from the previous grade's teachers exactly what the students were taught and the extent to which they mastered it, we have no practical way to gather artifacts and triangulate causes of the gaps. Therefore, when teams use pre-test data as the entry point into the model, their next step is to identify the learning gaps—there are no instructional gaps, at least not yet—and articulate a Target Learning Goal (see Figure 12). From this point on, the steps in the Data Action Model proceed as usual: conduct a Strategies Search, develop a Data Action Plan, implement the plan in the classroom, and evaluate the results.

Many more questions will arise for teams beginning to use the Data Action Model. Although I have attempted to do so in part, no text can anticipate all of the nuanced possibilities that can occur with such complex work. Even teams in their second or third year of implementing the model have questions, encounter obstacles, and ride through bumpy spots. No model is perfect, no team is without issues, and no school can maintain a laser focus on its goals 100 percent of the time. But the Data Action Model helps teacher teams unite in their efforts to transform numbers into action and to make a difference for all students.

— Figure 12 —

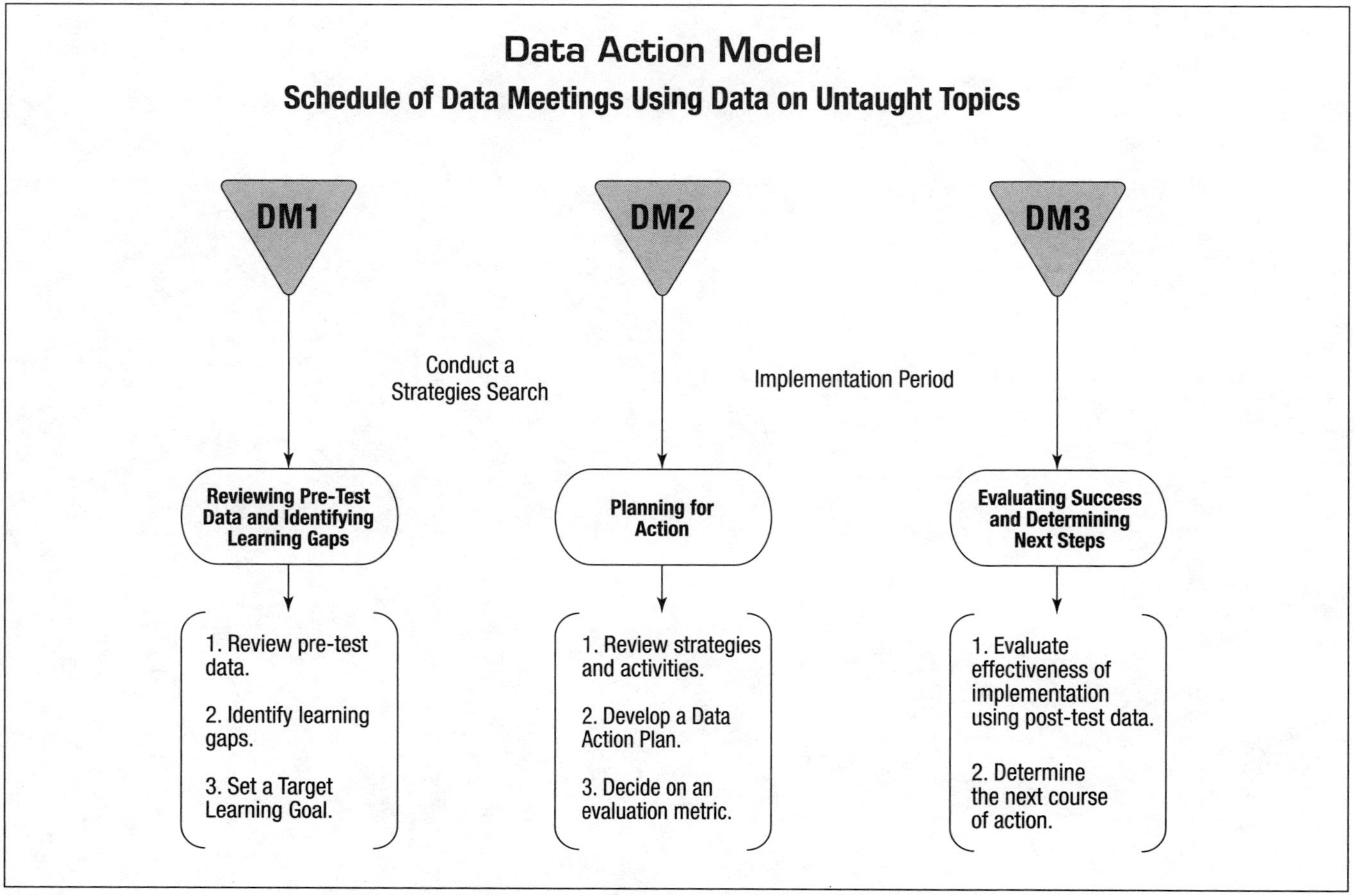
Data Action Model
Schedule of Data Meetings Using Data on Untaught Topics
DM1
DM2
DM3
Conduct a Strategies Search
Implementation Period
Reviewing Pre-Test Data and Identifying Learning Gaps
Planning for Action
Evaluating Success and Determining Next Steps
1. Review pre-test data.
2. Identify learning gaps.
3. Set a Target Learning Goal.
1. Review strategies and activities.
2. Develop a Data Action Plan.
3. Decide on an evaluation metric.
1. Evaluate effectiveness of implementation using post-test data.
2. Determine the next course of action.

Appendix

Protocols, Guides, and Tools

These documents can be downloaded at www.ascd.org/ASCD/pdf/books/venables2014.pdf. Use the password "venables114007" to unlock the PDF.

Notice and Wonder Protocol

Time: 40 minutes
Roles: Facilitator, timekeeper, recorder, participants

Step 1. Participants are presented with a table or graph of data pertaining to their practice. The data may be displayed on a screen for all to see, or they may be given to each PLC member in hard-copy form. (I prefer the former, since graphs and sometimes data in table form are often illustrated in color.)

Step 2. Each participant receives a 5-by-7-inch index card. Quietly and individually, participants write three or four observations evident in the graph or table. These observations must be free of inference or speculation; they are factual, based on objective examination of the display. Each observation starts with the phrase "I notice that . . .". (5 minutes)

Step 3. *Round 1:* In turn, each participant reads aloud one new observation that has not yet been shared, each time beginning with the phrase "I notice that . . .". The scribe records the responses on chart paper or in a Google Drive document. After the last participant shares one new observation, the first participant offers a second new observation, and the process continues until all observations have been shared aloud, *without discussion.* (5 minutes)

Step 4. Each participant turns over his or her index card and silently writes three or four speculations or question-statements based on the observations heard in Round 1. These speculations attempt to offer possible explanations for the observations or pose suggestions for pursuing additional data. No attempt should be made to solve the problems that surface; the intent is to gain insights into what the data suggest, how the data are connected, and what the data imply. Each speculation starts with the phrase "I wonder why . . . ," "I wonder if . . . ," "I wonder how . . . ," or "I wonder whether . . .". (5 minutes)

Step 5. *Round 2:* In turn, each participant reads aloud one new speculation that has not yet been shared, each time beginning with the phrase "I wonder . . .". The facilitator records the responses on chart paper. This process continues as in Round 1 until all speculations have been shared aloud, *without discussion,* except in cases where the facilitator chooses to ask follow-up questions to a teacher sharing a Wonder Statement or to the team. (10 minutes)

Step 6. The PLC discusses what has been shared and possible causes and connections to classroom instruction, and notes additional data that may be needed. (15 minutes)

Source: From *The Practice of Authentic PLCs: A Guide to Effective Teacher Teams* (pp. 157–158), by D. R. Venables, 2011, Thousand Oaks, CA: Corwin. © 2011 by Corwin. Reprinted with permission.

Planning Protocol

Time: 60 minutes
Roles: Facilitator, timekeeper, recorder, participants
Prework: At the end of a PLC planning meeting, the PLC identifies an upcoming topic to be taught, a single "power standard" from the state or Common Core standards.
Homework: PLC members gather existing lesson plans, instructional strategies, and activities they have used in the past in teaching the selected standard. In addition to bringing *existing* materials, each member of the PLC brings *one new* instructional activity or lesson component.

Step 1. Reviewing the Materials (15 minutes)

Quietly and individually, the PLC members review the instructional activities or lesson components brought to this meeting. As this is happening, members score each component they review using the rubric below. Teachers may ask brief clarifying questions of the owners of the activities, if questions arise, but no other discussion happens during this step. (*Note:* Every component should be reviewed by at least two teachers.)

Step 2. Scoring the Materials (25 minutes)

As a team, the PLC discusses and evaluates each instructional activity/lesson component brought to the meeting. The PLC uses the following questions as a guide in scoring the activities/components. (*Note:* During this step, teachers refrain from making suggestions to improve the materials.)

Alignment: Which component of this lesson best aligns to the standards? Why? What do we think mastery looks like for these standards?

Impact: How much learning is likely to result from this lesson? Is the gain significant? Where do students typically have trouble with these concepts, and why? Do the activities/components selected work better for one group or another? Why?

Depth: Are students being pushed (and guided) to think on a higher level? How do you know? Which components of this lesson push deeper thinking? Do the activities/components selected lend themselves to differentiation? How?

Dimension	1	2	3	4
Alignment to Standards	Barely or not at all aligned	Somewhat aligned	Mostly aligned	Completely aligned
Impact on Learning	Low impact	Medium-low impact	Medium-high impact	High impact
Student Engagement	Low student engagement likely	Moderate engagement for some students	Moderate engagement for most students	High engagement for most students
Depth of Knowledge	Recall	Skill/concept	Strategic reasoning	Extended reasoning
Technology Integration	Opportunities to integrate technology overlooked	Use of some technology	Effective and prominent use of technology	Effective and innovative use of technology
Teacher Friendliness		High maintenance (lots of materials and prep work)	Low maintenance (few materials and/or little prep work)	
Rigor and Relevance	Teacher works	Students work	Students think	Students think and work

Step 3. Suggesting Improvements (10 minutes)

In light of the ratings of lesson components discussed in Step 2, members of the PLC suggest improvements for any part of any lesson. The suggested improvements are discussed and recorded on chart paper or in a Google Drive document. Some questions to guide the team during this step include

- What's another way we might . . . ?
- What might happen if we . . . ?
- What is an appropriate CFU (check for understanding) for this piece?
- What other approaches would work for this piece?
- What is the purpose of having students do . . . ?

Step 4. Follow-Up (5 minutes)

The PLC members decide which components they will implement and who on the team is responsible for which tasks associated with implementation.

Step 5. Debrief (5 minutes)

Tuning Protocol

Overview

The Tuning Protocol was originally developed as a means for the five high schools in the Coalition of Essential Schools' Exhibitions Project to receive feedback and fine-tune their developing student assessment systems, including exhibitions, portfolios, and design projects. Recognizing the complexities involved in developing new forms of assessment, the project staff developed a facilitated process to support educators in sharing their students' work and, with colleagues, reflecting upon the lessons that are embedded there. This collaborative reflection helps educators to design and refine their assessment systems, as well as support higher-quality student performance. Since its trial run in 1992, the Tuning Protocol has been widely used and adapted for professional development purposes in and among schools across the United States.

To take part in the Tuning Protocol, educators bring samples of either their own work or their students' work on paper and, whenever possible, on video, as well as some of the materials they have created to support student performance, such as assignment descriptions and scoring rubrics. In a circle of about 6 to 10 "critical friends" (usually other educators), a facilitator guides the group through the process and keeps time. The presenting educator, or team of educators, describes the context for the student work (the task or project)—uninterrupted by questions or comments from participants.

Often, the presenter begins with a focusing question or area about which he or she would especially welcome feedback (for example, "Are you seeing evidence of persuasive writing in the students' work?"). Participants have time to examine the student work and ask clarifying questions. Then, with the presenter listening but silent, participants offer warm (supportive) and cool (challenging) feedback. Participants often frame their feedback as a question (for example, "How might the project be different if students chose their research topics?").

After this feedback is offered, the presenter has the opportunity, again uninterrupted, to reflect on the feedback and address any comments or questions he or she chooses. Finally, the facilitator debriefs the experience. Both presenting and participating educators have found the Tuning experience to be a powerful stimulus for reflecting on their practice.

Source: From "Tuning Protocol: Overview," by T. Blythe, D. Allen, and B. S. Powell. © by National School Reform Faculty. Reprinted with permission. Available: www.nsrfharmony.org/protocol/doc/tuning.pdf

The Tuning Protocol

Time: 65–70 minutes
Roles: Presenter, facilitator, participants

Step 1. Introduction (5 minutes)

- Facilitator briefly introduces protocol goals, guidelines, and schedule.
- Participants briefly introduce themselves (if necessary).

Step 2. Presentation (15 minutes)

During this time, participants are silent; no questions are entertained. The presenter has an opportunity to share the context for the student work, including

- Information about the students and/or the class (what the students tend to be like, where they are in school, where they are in the year).
- Assignment or prompt that generated the student work.
- Student learning goals or standards that inform the work.

• Samples of student work (e.g., photocopies of work, video clips) with student names removed.

• Evaluation format (e.g., scoring rubric, assessment criteria).

• Focusing question for feedback.

Step 3. Clarifying Questions (5 minutes)

• Participants have an opportunity to ask clarifying questions to get additional information that they believe would help them understand the context for the student work. Clarifying questions are matters of "fact."

• The facilitator should be sure to limit the questions to those that are "clarifying," judging which questions more properly belong in the warm/cool feedback step.

Step 4. Examination of Student Work Samples (15 minutes)

• Participants look closely at the work, taking notes on where it seems to be in tune with the stated goals and where there might be problems. Participants focus particularly on the presenter's focusing question.

• Presenter is silent; participants do this work silently.

Step 5. Pause to Reflect on Warm and Cool Feedback (2–3 minutes)

• Participants take a couple of minutes to reflect on what they would like to contribute to the feedback session.

• Presenter is silent; participants do this work silently.

Step 6. Warm and Cool Feedback (15 minutes)

• Participants share feedback with one another while the presenter is silent. The feedback generally begins with a few minutes of warm feedback, moves on to a few minutes of cool feedback (sometimes phrased in the form of reflective questions), and then moves back and forth between warm and cool feedback.

• Warm feedback may include comments about how the work presented seems to meet the desired goals; cool feedback may include possible disconnects or problems. Often, participants offer ideas or suggestions for strengthening the work presented.

- The facilitator may need to remind participants of the presenter's focusing question, which should be posted for all to see.
- Presenter is silent and takes notes.

Step 7. Reflection (5 minutes)

- Presenter speaks to whichever comments/questions he or she chooses while participants are silent.
- This is not a time for the presenter to mount a defense but a time to reflect aloud on the ideas or questions that seemed particularly interesting or significant.
- Facilitator may intervene to focus, clarify, etc.

Step 8. Debrief (5 minutes)

- Facilitator leads a discussion of this Tuning experience.

Source: From "Tuning Protocol," by J. McDonald and D. Allen. © by National School Reform Faculty. Reprinted with permission. Available: www.nsrfharmony.org/protocol/doc/tuning.pdf

Consultancy Protocol

Overview

A Consultancy is a structured process for helping an individual or a team think more expansively about a particular, concrete dilemma. Outside perspective is critical to this protocol working effectively; therefore, some of the participants in the group must be people who do not share the presenter's specific dilemma at that time. When putting together a Consultancy group, be sure to include people with differing perspectives.

Framing Consultancy Dilemmas and Focus Questions

A dilemma is a puzzle, an issue that raises questions, an idea that seems to have conceptual gaps, or something about process or product that you just can't figure out. Sometimes it will include samples of student or adult work that illustrate the dilemma, but often it is a dilemma that crosses over many parts of the educational process.

Step 1. Think about your dilemma. Dilemmas involve issues with which you are struggling or that you are unsure about. The following questions will help you decide if it's a dilemma to bring to the Consultancy group:

- Is it something that is bothering you enough that your thoughts regularly return to it?
- Is it *not* already on its way to being resolved?
- Does it *not* depend on getting other people to change (in other words, can you affect the dilemma by changing your own practice)?

• Is it something that is important to you, and is it something you are willing to work on?

Step 2. Do some reflective writing about your dilemma. The following questions will help you reflect:

• Why is this a dilemma for you? Why is this dilemma important to you?

• If you could take a snapshot of this dilemma, what would you/we see?

• What have you done already to try to remedy or manage the dilemma?

• What have been the results of those attempts?

• Who do you hope will change? Who do you hope will take action to resolve this dilemma? If your answer is not you, you need to change your focus and present a dilemma that is about your practice, actions, behaviors, beliefs, and assumptions, and not someone else's.

• What do you assume to be true about this dilemma, and how have these assumptions influenced your thinking about the dilemma?

• What is your focus question? A focus question summarizes your dilemma and helps focus the feedback (see Step 3).

Step 3. Frame a focus question for your Consultancy group—that is, put your dilemma into question format, guided by the following:

• Try to pose a question around the dilemma that seems to get to the heart of the matter.

• Remember that the question you pose will guide the Consultancy group in its discussion of the dilemma.

Step 4. Critique your focus question. Ask yourself,

• Is this question important to my practice?

• Is this question important to student learning?

• Is this question important to others in my profession?

Some Examples of Dilemmas and Focus Questions

Dilemma: The teaching staff seems to love the idea of involving students in meaningful learning that connects them to real issues and an authentic audience beyond school, but in reality, nothing seems to be happening.

Focus question: What can I do to capitalize on teachers' interest and help them translate theory into practice?

Dilemma: The community is participating in visioning work, but the work doesn't seem to relate to the actual life of the school; it is just too utopian.

Focus question: How do I mesh dreams and reality?

Dilemma: Teachers love doing projects with students, but the projects never seem to connect to one another or have coherent educational goals or focus; they are just fun.

Focus question: How do I work with teachers to help them better foster deep learning about important concepts while still engaging students in hands-on learning?

Dilemma: We keep getting grants to do specific projects with students and the community, but when the money is gone, the work doesn't continue.

Focus question: How does sustainability actually work? What needs to change for it to work?

Dilemma: No matter how hard I try to be inclusive and ask for everyone's ideas, about half of the people don't want to try anything new—they think things were just fine before.

Focus question: How do I work with people who don't want to change without alienating them?

Preparing to Present a Dilemma in a Consultancy Protocol

Come to the session with a description of a dilemma related to your practice. Write your dilemma with as much contextual description as you feel you need for understanding. One page is generally sufficient; even half a page is often enough. If you prefer not to write it out, you can make notes for yourself and make an oral presentation, but please do some preparation ahead of time.

End your description of the dilemma with a specific focus question. Frame your question thoughtfully: what do you *really* want to know? What is your real dilemma? This question will help your Consultancy group focus its feedback. Avoid closed-ended (yes-or-no) questions, which generally yield less feedback.

Dilemmas involve any issues you are struggling with in your work, such as strategies that are problematic or have not been as effective as you would like. Consultancies give presenters an opportunity to tap the expertise in a group, and if past experiences offer any indication, you will be able to rely on the people in your Consultancy group to provide respectful, thoughtful, experience-based responses to your dilemma.

A couple of caveats: we have found that Consultancies don't go well when presenters bring dilemmas that are already well on their way to being resolved or that require people other than the presenter to change. To get the most out of this experience, bring an issue that is still puzzling you about your practice. It is riskier, but we guarantee that you will learn more.

The Consultancy Protocol

Time: Approximately 50 minutes
Roles: Presenter (participant whose work is being discussed by the group), facilitator (who sometimes participates, depending on the size of the group), participants

Step 1. The presenter gives an overview of the dilemma with which he or she is struggling and frames a focus question for the Consultancy group to consider. The framing of this question, as well as the quality of the presenter's reflection on the dilemma being discussed, are key features of this protocol. If the presenter has brought student work, educator work, or other "artifacts," there is a pause here to silently examine the work/documents. The focus of the group's conversation is on the dilemma. (5–10 minutes)

Step 2. The Consultancy group asks clarifying questions of the presenter—that is, questions that have brief, factual answers. (5 minutes)

Step 3. The Consultancy group asks probing questions of the presenter. These questions should be worded in a way that prompts the presenter to clarify and expand his or her thinking about the dilemma. The goal here is for the presenter to learn more about the question he or she framed or to analyze the dilemma. The presenter may respond to the Consultancy group's questions, but there is no discussion among the group of the presenter's responses. At the end of this step, the facilitator asks the presenter to restate his or her focus question for the group. (10 minutes)

Step 4. The Consultancy group members discuss the dilemma presented. (15 minutes)

Questions to frame the group discussion may include

- What did we hear?
- What didn't we hear that might be relevant?
- What assumptions seem to be operating?
- What questions does the dilemma raise for us?
- What do we think about the dilemma?
- What might we do or try if faced with a similar dilemma? What have we done in similar situations?

Members of the group sometimes suggest actions the presenter might consider taking. Most often, however, they work to define the issues more thoroughly and objectively. The presenter doesn't speak during this discussion but instead listens and takes notes.

Step 5. The presenter reflects on what he or she heard and is now thinking, sharing with the group anything that particularly resonated during any part of the Consultancy. (5 minutes)

Step 6. The facilitator leads a brief conversation about the group's observation of the Consultancy process. (5 minutes)

Facilitation Tips

1. The success of the Consultancy often depends on the quality of the presenter's reflection in Step 1 as well as on the quality and authenticity of the focus question framed for the Consultancy group. However, it is not uncommon for the presenter, at the end of a Consultancy, to say, "Now I know what my real question is." That is fine, too. It can be helpful for the presenter to prepare ahead of time a brief (one- to two-page) written description of the dilemma and related issues for the Consultancy group to read as part of Step 1.

2. Clarifying questions are for the person asking them. They ask the presenter *who, what, where, when,* or *how*—they are not *why* questions. They can be answered quickly and succinctly.

3. Probing questions are for the person answering them. They ask the presenter *why* (among other things) and are open-ended. They take longer to answer than clarifying questions and often require the presenter to think deeply before speaking.

4. When the group talks while the presenter listens, it is helpful for the presenter to pull his or her chair back away from the group. This protocol asks the Consultancy group to talk about the presenter in the third person. As awkward as this may feel at first, it often opens up a rich conversation, and it gives the presenter an opportunity to listen and take notes, without needing to respond to the group in any way. Remember that it is the group's job to offer an analysis of the dilemma or question presented. It is not necessary to solve the dilemma or to offer a definitive answer.

It is important for the presenter to listen in a nondefensive manner. Listen for new ideas, perspectives, and approaches. Listen to the group's analysis of your questions/issues. Listen for assumptions—both your own and the group's—implicit in the conversation. Don't listen for judgment of you by the group. This is not supposed to be about you but about a question you have raised. Remember that you asked the group to help you with this dilemma.

5. The point of this step is not for the presenter to give a blow-by-blow response to the group's conversation, nor is it to mount a defense or further explanation. Instead, this is a time for the presenter to talk about what he or she thought were the most significant comments, ideas, and questions offered. The presenter can also share any new thoughts or questions he or she had during the group's discussion.

6. Debriefing the process is key. Don't shortchange this step.

Source: From "Consultancy Protocol," by G. Thompson-Grove, P. Evans, and F. Dunne. © by National School Reform Faculty. Reprinted with permission. Available: www.nsrfharmony.org/protocol/doc/consultancy.pdf

PLC Coach's Guide to Asking Deeper Questions

The role of the PLC coach/facilitator involves much more than simply delineating the agenda or leading PLC members through the steps of a timely protocol. Although these tasks have their place and are part of the PLC coach's "job description," they do not actually lead the PLC to do work that has a significant impact on student learning.

To truly improve the work of the collective PLC and of individual teachers, PLC coaches must make a habit of asking probing, difficult questions. Without addressing deeper questions, the team is just a group of teachers who go through a series of motions that have been approved as proper practices of a PLC, but who do nothing to improve student learning. The last thing busy teachers need is to participate in meetings that, in the end, do nothing real or significant to foster their students' learning.

I developed this guide to help PLC coaches go deeper and push their PLC members to go deeper, so that they can make significant strides in instructional improvement. If PLCs are to do authentic, substantive work, PLC coaches must not only ask deeper questions and prompt PLC members to think on a deeper level but also relentlessly pursue asking these deeper questions. In my experience, this does not happen unless the PLC coach is aware of the importance of asking deeper questions and knows what such questions might look like.

Deeper questions

- Are general and widely useful, often transcending the current context in which they are addressed.
- Allow for multiple responses.
- Help create a paradigm shift in the thinking of individuals and teams.
- Empower individuals and teams to think more expansively about a topic, an issue, or a dilemma.
- Avoid closed-ended responses.
- Elicit slow, thoughtful responses.
- Move thinking from reaction to reflection, from being reactive to proactive.
- Encourage taking another person's perspective.

Some general question stems that help push deeper thinking include

- Why do you think this is the case?
- What would you have to change in order for . . . ?
- What do you feel is right in your gut?
- What do you wish . . . ?
- What's another way you might . . . ?
- What would it look like if . . . ?
- What do you think would happen if . . . ?
- How was [*ABC*] different from [*XYZ*]?
- What sort of impact do you think [*ABC*] would have on [*XYZ*]?
- What criteria did you use to . . . ?
- When have you done/experienced something like this before?
- What might you see happening in your classroom if . . . ?
- How did you determine that [*XYZ*] was best?
- What is your hunch about . . . ?
- What was your intention when . . . ?

- What do you assume to be true about . . . ?
- What is the connection between [*ABC*] and [*XYZ*]?
- What if the opposite were true? What would happen?
- How might your assumptions about [*ABC*] have influenced how you were thinking about [*XYZ*]?
- Why is this such a dilemma for you?

Some question stems that help push data conversations include

- What do you think that implies?
- Do you think we have evidence to support that statement? Where?
- Can you point to specific evidence?
- Why? How do you know?
- Do you think this is something that is systemic or specific to particular student populations?
- What do you think we should do to address that?
- What are the big issues here, as opposed to the secondary or ancillary issues?
- Can we see root causes, based on the evidence, that give rise to secondary symptoms in the issues we're seeing? What are the root causes?

When team members address deeper questions, important truths about instructional practice come to light. It's not that teachers have been hiding anything; it's more that they have not spent adequate time really looking at what they do and, more important, at the effect of their actions on student learning. It is the PLC coach's job to push this kind of questioning so that these truths bubble to the surface during discourse. The questions and question stems in this guide can help.

Developed in part with examples from NSRF's *Guide to Probing Questions* and Charlotte Danielson's *Pathwise ~ Mediational Questions.*

Shared Dilemma Protocol

Purpose: Often, teacher teams experience dilemmas or problems that are pervasive across a grade level or subject area. This protocol provides a structured way for teacher teams to start the process of solving a shared dilemma or problem that is within their sphere of influence or control.

Time: Approximately 60 minutes

Roles: Facilitator (explains each step/moderates and participates), time-keeper, recorder, participants

Prework: In a prior meeting, the PLC identifies a specific and highly focused dilemma that most members are facing.

Step 1. The Dilemma

The group reviews a common dilemma or question. Participants may ask a few clarifying questions to be sure everyone at the table has necessary information. (5 minutes)

Step 2. Probing Questions

a. Each participant takes three minutes to quietly write down one probing question that will encourage deeper conversations about the dilemma. Participants share their questions in turn, without discussion. The recorder writes them on chart paper, on a whiteboard, or in a digital format that everyone can see. (10 minutes)

b. Participants take time to respond to and discuss some or all of the probing questions on the list. The recorder writes the responses where everyone can see them. (10 minutes)

Step 3. Solutions

a. Participants brainstorm possible solutions together. The recorder writes the ideas where everyone can see them. (10 minutes)

b. Participants have an open discussion about the proposed solutions and are encouraged to ask clarifying questions to gain a better understanding of the proposed solutions. (10 minutes)

Step 4. Next Steps

The facilitator asks questions like "What will we do now based on this discussion?" "Which solutions would you like to put into an action plan?" and "Which solutions would you like to investigate further?" The recorder takes notes with the intention to share them with the group via e-mail or uses the chart below to organize ideas. (10 minutes)

Solutions requiring investigation	Time line	Responsible party	Solutions to put into action	Time line	Responsible party

Step 5. Debrief (5 minutes)

Source: From "Shared Dilemma Protocol v. 1.3," by C. Begin, 2013. © 2013 by Cari Begin. Reprinted with permission.

Text-Based Seminar

Text-Based Seminar Guidelines

Purpose: Enlargement of understanding of a text, *not* the achievement of some particular understanding.

Ground rules:

- Refer to the text, and challenge others to go to the text. Use page numbers. Wait for others to get to the quote, then read it aloud.
- Listen actively.
- Build on what others say, referring to them by name.
- Don't step on others' talk. Allow for silences and pauses. Make time and space so everyone can participate.
- Converse directly with one another, and let the conversation flow as much as possible—without raising hands or using a speaker's list.
- Make the assumptions underlying your comments explicit to others.
- Ask questions of others to build understanding.
- Watch your own airtime—in terms of both how often you speak and how much you say when you speak.

Notes to Text-Based Seminar Facilitators

Text-Based Seminars can be remarkably engaging and productive for both students and adults. A Text-Based Seminar facilitator has two primary tasks: posing the framing question and keeping the group focused without pushing any particular agenda.

Facilitating a seminar is not terribly difficult, but it can be challenging. A few tips might make the job easier:

1. Invest time in creating the framing question. It needs to be substantive, clear, relevant to the participants' experience, and likely to push their thinking in new directions. Above all, constructing a response to the question should require close reading of the text. We recommend that the framing question be genuine for everyone, including the facilitator, so that the entire group is engaged in the inquiry. Framing questions are often based on a quote from the text, which begins to establish a pattern of using the document as a basis for the conversation.

2. In addition to the framing question, create a few follow-up questions that seem to raise the level of participants' thinking. If the group takes off, you may never use them (or you may create new ones that come from the conversation itself), but it's a good idea to have something in your hip pocket, especially if you aren't very experienced at this kind of facilitation.

3. Unless the entire group routinely engages in Text-Based Seminars, it is useful to go over the purposes and ground rules before you begin. Because so many conversations (in school and out) are based more on opinion than on evidence, and aim toward winning the argument rather than constructing new knowledge, it is important to remind the group of the basics: *work from the text* and *strive to enlarge your understanding.*

4. Give the group time (about 10 minutes) to reread the text with the framing question in mind.

5. The most common facilitation problems in this kind of seminar come from two kinds of participants: those who need to win, and those who want to express opinions independent of the text and will use any quote they can find as a springboard. Usually, a reminder of the ground rules will pull them back in, although it is sometimes necessary to redirect the conversation. If you are dealing with a particularly insistent "winner," try asking the group to closely examine the assumptions underneath the arguments or opinions expressed. When someone doesn't stick to the text, it is often helpful to ask the group to look for evidence of the opinion being expressed in the text. What you don't want to do is ask these two types of participants a direct

question or invite them to cite the textual evidence that supports their opinions (although you might be tempted to do so). The goal is to redirect the conversation away from these folks, not to get them to talk more!

6. It can be useful to keep running notes of the conversation and to periodically summarize for the group what has been said.

7. It is also sometimes useful (especially if you are nervous) to have a "plant" among the participants—someone who will model ideal participant behavior at an early point in the seminar.

8. As is always the case when facilitating, try to keep the conversation balanced. Don't let one or two people dominate. If there are many quiet people, ask them to speak in pairs for a few minutes on a particular point to give them an entry into the larger conversation. Sometimes you just have to say, "Let's hear from someone who hasn't said much yet," and then use lots of wait time, even though it may feel uncomfortable to do so.

Source: From "Text-Based Seminar Guidelines," by G. Thompson-Grove. © by National School Reform Faculty. Reprinted with permission. Available: www.nsrfharmony.org/protocol/doc/text_based_guidelines.pdf

Four *A*s Text Protocol

Step 1. The group reads the text silently, highlighting it and writing notes on sticky notes in response to the following four questions (you can also add your own *A*s):

- What **assumptions** does the author of the text hold?
- What do you **agree** with in the text?
- What do you want to **argue** with in the text?
- What parts of the text do you **aspire** to?

Step 2. In a round, have each person identify one assumption in the text, citing the text (with page numbers, if appropriate) as evidence.

Step 3. Either continue in rounds or facilitate a conversation in which the group talks about the text in light of each of the remaining *A*s, taking them one at a time—what do people agree with, argue with, and aspire to in the text? Try to move seamlessly from one *A* to the next, giving each one enough time for full exploration.

Step 4. End the session with an open discussion framed around a question such as "What does this mean for our work with students?"

Step 5. Debrief the experience.

Source: From "Four 'A's' Text Protocol," by J. Gray, 2005. © by National School Reform Faculty. Reprinted with permission. Available: www.nsrfharmony.org/protocol/doc/4_a_text.pdf

The Final Word

Purpose: The purpose of this discussion format is to give all members of the group an opportunity to have their ideas, understandings, and perspective enhanced by hearing from others. With this format, the group members can explore an article or other text, clarify their thinking, and question their assumptions and beliefs to gain a deeper understanding of the issue.
Roles: Facilitator/timekeeper (who also participates), participants
Facilitation: Have participants identify one "most" significant idea from the text (underlined or highlighted ahead of time), stick to the time limits, avoid dialogue, and work in equal-sized circles so that all small groups finish at approximately the same time.
Time: For each round, allow about 8 minutes (e.g., for circles of five participants, the presenter gets 3 minutes, the four responders get 1 minute each, and the presenter gets 1 minute for the final word). The role of the facilitator is to keep the process moving and clearly connected to the text, and to keep time so that everyone gets an opportunity for a round. For a group of five, the total time for this process should be approximately 40 minutes.

The Process

Step 1. Sit in a circle, and identify a facilitator/timekeeper.

Step 2. Each person needs to have one "most" significant idea from the text underlined or highlighted. It is often helpful to identify a backup quote as well.

Step 3. The first person begins by reading what struck him or her the most from the text. Have this person refer to where the quote is in the text—one thought or quote only. Then, in less than 3 minutes, this person describes why that quote struck him or her. For example, why does he or she agree/disagree with the quote, what questions does he or she have about that quote, what issues does it raise for him or her, and what does he or she now wonder about in relation to that quote?

Step 4. Continuing around the circle, each person responds to that quote and what the presenter said in under a minute. The purpose of the response is to

- Expand on the presenter's thinking about the quote and the issues raised for him or her by the quote;
- Provide a different look at the quote;
- Clarify the presenter's thinking about the quote; or
- Question the presenter's assumptions about the quote and the issues raised (although at this time there is no response from the presenter).

Step 5. After going around the circle with each person having responded in under a minute, the original presenter takes a minute to have the "final word": what is he or she thinking? What is his or her reaction to what the circle members have said?

Step 6. The cycle continues, with the next person in the circle sharing what struck him or her most from the text. Proceed around the circle, responding to each subsequent presenter's quote in the same way. This process continues until each person has had a round.

Step 7. The facilitator in each circle debriefs the process.

Source: From "The Final Word," adapted by J. Fisher-Mueller and G. Thompson-Grove for NSRF. © by National School Reform Faculty. Reprinted with permission. Available: www.nsrfharmony.org/protocol/doc/final_word.pdf

10 Potential Data Discussion Pitfalls* and How to React to Them

*aka *Opportunities*

If Your Teacher Team Does This	You Ask/Say This
Focus of data conversation shifts to issues over which the team has no control.	*We have no real control over [XYZ]. But given those challenges, what can we do about [XYZ]?*
Focus of data conversation is on trivial, relatively unimportant observations.	*So what does this imply for [XYZ]? How does this affect the big picture? What generalizations can you draw from these observations? If you were to rank these items by priority, what would your list look like?*
Teacher team is quick to blame students and reluctant to accept responsibility for learning gaps.	*What could we be doing that we're not already doing? What part of this are we responsible for? What action should we take to improve this?*
Data conversation becomes micro-focused on one particular student or test item.	*So what does this imply for all of our students? What general observations do you have that affect most of our students? Do you think this is representative of all students [or all test items]?*
Focus of data conversation shifts to skills students "should have acquired before this year."	*So what can we do? How can we provide support for students who lack prerequisite skills? What about students who do have these skills?*
Teacher team jumps prematurely to proposing solutions.	*Part of this process is refraining from deciding on solutions until all relevant information has been presented and analyzed. Let's continue to get information that is relevant and hold back from proposing solutions until we have a clearer picture of what is going on.*
Focus of data conversation shifts to items unrelated to the data at hand.	*Let's make sure that we base our comments on the evidence before us. What evidence do we have? What does it tell us about student learning?*
Focus of data conversation is on secondary symptoms of an undiscussed primary issue.	*What could be the root cause of this issue?*
Teacher team is celebratory and self-congratulatory about what is working.	*It's great that the students are doing so well on [XYZ]. What can we apply from this success to some of the areas where students are still struggling?*
Focus of data conversation shifts to sustained sentiments of helplessness and pessimism.	*It's frustrating when students don't perform the way we want them to. What are some aspects we do have control over?*

Source: From "10 Potential Data Discussion Pitfalls," by D. R. Venables and N. Cooperman, 2013. © 2013 by Daniel R. Venables and Teaching Matters, Inc. Reprinted with permission.

Artifact Tracking Sheet

Artifact Type (be specific) • Data table • Student work • Teacher lesson plan(s) • Teacher instruction calendar • Test items • Unit plan	**Observed Learning Gap** (as evidenced by artifact) ***or*** **Observed Instructional Gap** (as evidenced by artifact)	**Relative Significance** (if learning gap observed) *How important is this skill/concept?*	**Prominence** (if learning gap observed) *Speculate as to how widespread this gap is with all the students.*
	LG IG	1 2 3 4 5	1 2 3 4 5
	LG IG	1 2 3 4 5	1 2 3 4 5
	LG IG	1 2 3 4 5	1 2 3 4 5
	LG IG	1 2 3 4 5	1 2 3 4 5
	LG IG	1 2 3 4 5	1 2 3 4 5
	LG IG	1 2 3 4 5	1 2 3 4 5
	LG IG	1 2 3 4 5	1 2 3 4 5
	LG IG	1 2 3 4 5	1 2 3 4 5
	LG IG	1 2 3 4 5	1 2 3 4 5
	LG IG	1 2 3 4 5	1 2 3 4 5

Action Plan Tracking Sheet

GOAL:					
Instructional Tactic (be specific) *What will be done?*	**Tactic Method** *Specifically how will it be done?*	**Acting Party** *Who will do it?*	**Frequency** *How often will this task be done?*	**Completion Date**	**Verifying Artifacts** Which artifacts will serve as evidence that the instructional tactic has been implemented?
Evaluation Metric					

Bibliography

Ainsworth, L., & Viegut, D. (2006). *Common formative assessments: How to connect standards-based instruction and assessment.* Thousand Oaks, CA: Corwin Press.

Bambrick-Santoyo, P. (2009). *Driven by data: A practical guide to improve instruction.* San Francisco: Wiley.

Begin, C. (2013). Shared dilemma protocol.

Blythe, T., Allen, D., & Powell, B. S. (n.d.). Tuning protocol: Overview. Bloomington, IN: National School Reform Faculty. Available: www.nsrfharmony.org/protocol/doc/tuning.pdf

Boudett, K. P., City, E. A., & Murnane, R. J. (2005). *Data wise: A step-by-step guide to using assessment results to improve teaching and learning.* Cambridge, MA: Harvard Education Press.

Boudett, K., & Steele, J. (2007). *Data wise in action: Stories of schools using data to improve teaching and learning.* Cambridge, MA: Harvard Education Press.

Brookhart, S. M. (2009). The many meanings of "multiple measures." *Educational Leadership, 67*(3), 6–12.

Brown, L. E. (2009). *Protocols for professional learning.* Alexandria, VA: ASCD.

Buffum, A., Mattos, M., & Weber, C. (2008). *Pyramid response to intervention.* Bloomington, IN: Solution Tree.

Chappuis, S., Chappuis, J., & Stiggins, R. (2009, February). Supporting teacher learning teams. *Educational Leadership, 66*(5), 56–60.

Curtis, R. E., & City, E. A. (2009). *Strategy in action: How school systems can support powerful learning and teaching.* Cambridge, MA: Harvard Education Press.

Doran, G. T., Miller, A., & Cunningham, J. (1981, November). There's a S.M.A.R.T. way to write management's goals and objectives. *Management Review, 70*(11).

DuFour, R., DuFour, R., Eaker, R., & Many, T. (2006). *Learning by doing: A handbook for professional learning communities at work.* Bloomington, IN: Solution Tree.

Dukic, V. M., Lopes, H. F., & Polson, N. (2009, November 25). Tracking epidemics with state-space SEIR and Google flu trends. *Social Science Research Network.* Retrieved July 6, 2013, from http://papers.ssrn.com/sol3/papers.cfm?abstract_id=1513705

Easton, L. B. (2009). *Protocols for professional learning.* Alexandria, VA: ASCD.

Evans, R. (2001). *The human side of school change: Reform, resistance, and the real-life problems of innovation.* Jossey-Bass Education Series. San Francisco: Jossey-Bass.

Fisher-Mueller, J., & Thompson-Grove, G. (n.d.). The final word. Bloomington, IN: National School Reform Faculty. Available: nsrfharmony.org/protocol/doc/final_word.pdf

Fullan, M. (2001). *Leading in a culture of change.* San Francisco: Jossey-Bass.

Gray, J. (2005). Four "*A's*" text protocol. Bloomington, IN: National School Reform Faculty. Available: www.nsrfharmony.org/protocol/doc/4_a_text.pdf

Gregory, G. H., & Kuzmich, L. (2004). *Data driven differentiation in the standards-based classroom*. Thousand Oaks, CA: Corwin Press.

Hargreaves, A., & Fullan, M. (2012). *Professional capital: Transforming teaching in every school*. New York: Teachers College Press.

Hord, S., & Hirsh, S. (2009). The principal's role in supporting learning communities. *Educational Leadership, 66*(5), 22–23.

Hord, S., & Sommers, W. (2008). *Leading professional learning communities*. Thousand Oaks, CA: Corwin Press.

James-Ward, C., Fisher, D., Frey, N., & Lapp D. (2013). *Using data to focus instructional improvement*. Alexandria, VA: ASCD.

Love, N. (2009). *Using data to improve learning for all: A collaborative inquiry approach*. Thousand Oaks, CA: Corwin Press.

Mayer-Schönberger, V., & Cukier, K. (2013). *Big data: A revolution that will transform how we live, work, and think*. Boston: Houghton Mifflin Harcourt.

McDonald, J., & Allen, D. (n.d.). Tuning protocol. Bloomington, IN: National School Reform Faculty. Available: www.nsrfharmony.org/protocol/doc/tuning.pdf

McDonald, J., Mohr, N., Dichter, A., & McDonald, E. C. (2007). *The power of protocols: An educator's guide to better practice* (2nd ed.). New York: Teachers College Press.

Ortquist-Ahrens, L., & Torosyan, R. (2009). The role of the facilitator in faculty learning communities: Paving the way for growth, productivity, and collegiality. *Learning Communities Journal, 1*(1), 29–62.

Patterson, K., Grenny, J., McMillan, R., & Switzler, A. (2002). *Crucial conversations: Tools for talking when stakes are high*. New York: McGraw-Hill.

Reeves, D. (2006). *The learning leader*. Alexandria, VA: ASCD.

Reeves, D. B. (2004). *Accountability for learning: How teachers and school leaders can take charge*. Alexandria, VA: ASCD.

Ruebel, K. K. (2012). *AMLE research summary: Professional learning communities*. Westerville, OH: Association for Middle Level Education.

Smith, D., Wilson, B., & Corbett, D. (2009, February). How teachers learn: Moving beyond talk. *Educational Leadership*. Retrieved May 6, 2013, from www.ascd.org/publications/educational-leadership/feb09/vol66/num05/Moving-Beyond-Talk.aspx

Stiggins, R. (2001). *Student involved classroom assessment* (3rd ed.). Upper Saddle River, NJ: Prentice-Hall.

Thompson-Grove, G. (n.d.). Text-based seminar guidelines. Bloomington, IN: National School Reform Faculty. Available: www.nsrfharmony.org/protocol/doc/text_based_guidelines.pdf

Thompson-Grove, G., Evans, P., & Dunne, F. (n.d.). Consultancy protocol. Bloomington, IN: National School Reform Faculty. Available: www.nsrfharmony.org/protocol/doc/consultancy.pdf

Tomlinson, C. A. (2004). *How to differentiate instruction in mixed-ability classrooms* (2nd ed.). Alexandria, VA: ASCD.

Venables, D. R. (2011). *The practice of authentic PLCs: A guide to effective teacher teams*. Thousand Oaks, CA: Corwin Press.

Venables, D. R., & Cooperman, N. (2013). 10 potential data discussion pitfalls. New York: Teaching Matters, Inc.

Vescio, V., Ross, D., & Adams, A. (2008). A review of research on the impact of professional learning communities on teaching practice and student learning. *Teaching and Teacher Education, 24*(1), 80–91.

Index

Note: Page references followed by an italicized *f* indicate information contained in figures.

About the Author

Daniel R. Venables is founder and executive director of the Center for Authentic PLCs (www.authenticPLCs.com), an independent consulting firm committed to assisting schools in building, leading, and sustaining authentic PLCs. He is the author of *The Practice of Authentic PLCs: A Guide to Effective Teacher Teams* (Corwin Press, 2011). During his career of more than 30 years in education, Daniel has been a classroom teacher in both public and independent schools in South Carolina, North Carolina, and Connecticut for 24 years, serving as a math department chair for 18 of those years. He was Professional Development Coordinator with the nation's 18th-largest district, Charlotte-Mecklenburg Schools.

Daniel holds a master's degree in mathematics from Wesleyan University. In 1994, he was trained as a Math/Science Fellow with the Coalition of Essential Schools (CES), where he began his working experience with PLCs. In 2002, he was named South Carolina Independent School Teacher of the Year.

In addition to working directly with schools and faculties to offer on-site, ongoing, sustained support, he also presents regularly at national and regional educational conferences. Several times a year, he sponsors a three-day PLC coach training program throughout the United States called the Grapple Institutes. To learn more about the Grapple Institutes, visit http://authenticplcs.com. To invite Daniel to your school or inquire about hosting a Grapple Institute at your school, contact him at dvenables@authenticplcs.com or call 803-206-3578.

Related ASCD Resources: Using Data to Improve Teaching and Learning

At the time of publication, the following ASCD resources were available (ASCD stock numbers appear in parentheses). For up-to-date information about ASCD resources, go to www.ascd.org. You can search the complete archives of *Educational Leadership* at http://www.ascd.org/el.

Professional Interest Communities
Visit the ASCD website and scroll to the bottom to click on "professional interest communities." Within these communities, find information about professional educators who have formed groups around topics like "Common Core in the Classroom" and "Professional Learning Communities."

ASCD EDge Groups
Exchange ideas and connect with other educators interested in various topics, including PLCs and Action Research and PLCs, on the social networking site ASCD EDge™.

PD Online
Schools as Professional Learning Communities: An Introduction (#PD09OC28)
Using Data to Determine Student Mastery (#PD14OC001)

These and other online courses are available at www.ascd.org/pdonline

Print Products
The Art and Science of Teaching: A Comprehensive Framework for Effective Instruction by Robert J. Marzano (#107001)
Classroom Instruction That Works: Research-Based Strategies for Increasing Student Achievement (2nd ed.) by Ceri B. Dean, Elizabeth Hubbell, Howard Pitler, and Bj Stone (#111001)
The Curriculum Mapping Planner: Templates, Tools, and Resources for Effective Professional Development by Heidi Hayes Jacobs and Ann W. Johnson (#109010)
Enhancing Professional Practice: A Framework for Teaching (2nd ed.) by Charlotte F. Danielson (#106034)
Improving Teaching with Collaborative Action Research: An ASCD Action Tool by Diane Cunningham (#111006)
Making Standards Useful in the Classroom by Robert J. Marzano and Mark W. Haystead (#108006)
Strengthening and Enriching Your Professional Learning Community: The Art of Learning Together by Renate N. Caine and Geoffrey Caine (#110085)
Using Common Core Standards to Enhance Classroom Instruction and Assessment by Robert J. Marzano, Phil Warrick, Tammy Heflebower, David C. Yanoski, Julia A. Simms, and Jan K. Hoegh (#313066)
Using Data to Focus Instructional Improvement by Diane K. Lapp, Nancy E. Frey, Douglas B. Fisher, and Cheryl James-Ward (#113003)
What Works in Schools: Translating Research into Action by Robert J. Marzano (#102271)

DVDs
Enhancing Professional Practice DVD Series (#609033)
Examining Student Work (#601283)
Using Classroom Assessment to Guide Instruction (#602286)
A Visit to a Data-Driven School District (#606059)

The Whole Child Initiative
THE WHOLE CHILD The Whole Child Initiative helps schools and communities create learning environments that allow students to be healthy, safe, engaged, supported, and challenged. To learn more about other books and resources that relate to the whole child, visit www.wholechildeducation.org.

For more information: send e-mail to member@ascd.org; call 1-800-933-2723 or 703-578-9600, press 2; send a fax to 703-575-5400; or write to Information Services, ASCD, 1703 N. Beauregard St., Alexandria, VA 22311-1714 USA.

Cynthia Drummond